the little
book of
humanism

the little book of humanism

Universal lessons
on finding purpose,
meaning and joy

**Andrew Copson and
Alice Roberts**

PIATKUS

First published in Great Britain in 2020 by Piatkus

12

Text copyright © 2020 Andrew Copson and Alice Roberts

The moral right of the authors has been asserted.

A CIP catalogue record for this book is available from
the British Library.

ISBN 978 0 349 42546 7

Designed and typeset by EM&EN
Printed and bound in Great Britain by Clays Ltd, Elcograf S.p.A

Papers used by Piatkus are from well-managed forests
and other responsible sources.

PIATKUS
An imprint of
Little, Brown Book Group
Carmelite House
50 Victoria Embankment
London EC4Y 0DZ

An Hachette UK Company
www.hachette.co.uk
www.improvementzone.co.uk

*Dedicated to all those who
think for themselves
and act for others*

Contents

Welcome

Here's a secret that more and more people are discovering: you don't need religion to live a good life. The natural world is wonderful enough, without having to imagine a supernatural or divine dimension to it. And our natural human capacities for reason, kindness and love are all we need to live well and with meaning.

Throughout history there have been non-religious people who have believed that this life is the only life we have, that the universe is a natural phenomenon with no supernatural side, and that we can live ethical and fulfilling lives – using reason and humanity to guide us. These people have looked to scientific evidence and reason to understand the world. And they've placed human welfare and happiness – as well as the welfare of other sentient animals – at the heart of how they choose to live their life.

Today, people who hold these beliefs and values are called humanists. There are millions of individuals around the globe who share this way of living and of looking at the world – even if they haven't heard of the word 'humanism', and realised that it describes what they believe.

You might have heard of humanism before, or you might be reading this now and thinking: This describes me! I've been a humanist without even knowing it.

There are more humanists today than ever before, as the influence of religion wanes around the world. And many religious people are finding humanist ideas appealing – and religions themselves are changing as a result.

Humanism is a positive approach to life which has underpinned many of the humanitarian revolutions as well as the drive for equality over the last few centuries. That is something we should celebrate.

We wanted to share humanist ideas even more widely, and that's why we've written this book. We've collected together what we hope are inspiring and thought-provoking words from humanists – past and present – containing universal lessons on finding purpose, meaning and joy in our lives. The humanist tradition is dynamic and evolving – it's an ongoing conversation about how to live truthfully, ethically and happily. We hope this book will help you find a way to join that conversation.

Andrew Copson and Alice Roberts
October 2019

Hello babies. Welcome to Earth. It's hot in the summer and cold in the winter. It's round and wet and crowded. On the outside, babies, you've got a hundred years here. There's only one rule that I know of, babies – God damn it, you've got to be kind.

Kurt Vonnegut

children of earth

We are here because one odd group of fishes had a peculiar fin anatomy that could transform into legs for terrestrial creatures; because the earth never froze entirely during an ice age; because a small and tenuous species, arising in Africa a quarter of a million years ago, has managed, so far, to survive by hook and by crook.

Stephen Jay Gould

All the evidence points to the origin of our universe in a Big Bang, when matter was created out of energy, in a huge explosion nearly 14 billion years ago.

Much more recently – about 4.5 billion years ago – this planet formed out of molten debris orbiting around its star, our sun. Then, around a billion years later, the first life forms appeared.

Starting with single-celled organisms, millions of different species evolved here – and are still evolving. Many millions of species have become extinct, but there are still millions left, from bacteria to plants, and fungi to animals.

We are one of those species.

We are earthlings like every other life form on this planet.

Though below me, I feel no motion

Standing on these mountains and plains

Far away from the rolling ocean

Still my dry land heart can say

I've been sailing all my life now

Never harbor or port have I known

The wide universe is the ocean I travel

And the earth is my blue boat home

Peter Mayer

We humans are part of nature, not separate from it.

We're connected to every living thing on the planet.

If you feel a sense of quiet comfort in a green forest, or joy when the rain falls around you, or pleasure when the sun warms your face, you're feeling a deep and meaningful connection with your own natural environment.

Try to think about this next time you are outside in nature.

We are nestled in the story of life on this planet – part of it.

The humanist has a feeling of perfect at-homeness in the universe. He is conscious of himself as an earth-child. There is a mystic glow in this sense of belonging . . . Rooted in millions of years of planetary history, he has a secure feeling of being at home, and a consciousness of pride and dignity as a bearer of the heritage of the ages and growing creative centre of cosmic life.

Eustace Haydon

We could never have loved
the earth so well if we had
had no childhood in it, if it
were not the earth where the
same flowers come up again
every spring that we used to
gather with our tiny fingers
as we sat lisping to ourselves
on the grass . . .

George Eliot

India is famous as a land of many gods and goddesses. Historically, there was a wide diversity of beliefs there, just as there is today. India even had its own ancient humanists.

Known as the philosophers of the Charvaka (or Lokayata) school, and originally part of an oral tradition, their teachings were first written down around 2,600 years ago. Like modern scientists, they saw the universe as a natural phenomenon and human beings as part of nature:

> 'There is no heaven, no final liberation, no soul, no other world . . . How can this body, once dust or ashes, return?'

> 'Who paints the peacocks? Who makes the cuckoos sing? There is no cause of these things except nature.'

The original texts of the Charvaka school did not survive – we only know their words from later quotes. But we do know they were enormously influential. Some scholars of Indian philosophy believe their ideas may even have represented the secular 'common sense' of Indians of the day.

The twentieth-century Indian humanist M.N. Roy summed up the Charvaka philosophy:

> Morality is natural, it is a social convention and convenience, not a divine command. There is no need to control instincts and emotions; they are commands of nature. The purpose of life is to live; and the only wisdom is happiness.

For humanists, the question of *why* we are here is not a real question.

There is no direction or purpose to the universe; no 'why' in that sense.

Human beings often do things with purposes in mind, with aims and ends in view. But the moon, the sun, the stars – and the universe as a whole, with all the natural processes that occur in it – are not the sort of things that can have purposes, aims and ends in mind.

Realising that there is no 'why', that there is no higher reason for our existence, liberates us to create our own meaning in our lives.

I use the word humanist to mean someone
who believes that man is just as much a
natural phenomenon as an animal or a plant,
that his body, his mind, and his soul were not
supernaturally created but are all products of
evolution, and that he is not under the control or
guidance of any supernatural Being or beings,
but has to rely on himself and his own powers.

Julian Huxley

It doesn't make sense to ask *why* we are here, but it does make sense to ask *how* we came to be here.

The answer is an amazing story.

Our journey started deep in time and deep in the oceans, when a spark of life flickered into being. Just a few molecules clustering together, replicating, pulling a membrane around itself . . .

This was the beginning of all life on earth.

Then life unfurled, gathering pace and energy and complexity – spawning multicellular life forms, branching in many different directions, generating so many different species.

Endless forms most beautiful and most wonderful.

Generation by generation, forms changed, evolved. Getting closer to the present, we find ancestors who were fish, amphibians, reptiles, early mammals, early primates, apes – all the way to us, to humans.

We are the last human species to have evolved, around 300,000 years ago, in Africa.

I'd rather be a rising ape

than a falling angel.

Terry Pratchett

All the atoms that make up your body existed before you were conceived and will be there at the end, after you have gone.

I know that nothing is destructible; things merely change forms. When the consciousness we know as life ceases, I know that I shall still be part and parcel of the world. I was a part before the sun rolled into shape and burst forth in the glory of change. I was, when the earth was hurled out from its fiery rim. I shall return with the earth to Father Sun, and still exist in substance when the sun has lost its fire, and disintegrated into infinity to perhaps become a part of the whirling rubble of space. Why fear? The stuff of my being is matter, ever changing, ever moving, but never lost; so what need of denominations and creeds to deny myself the comfort of all my fellow men? The wide belt of the universe has no need for finger-rings. I am one with the infinite and need no other assurance.

Zora Neale Hurston

Feeling part of the universe can bring us closer to all other human beings as well.

This spiritual experience came one evening as I stood looking over the green ocean towards the red sunset. A great calm came over me. I became lost in the beauty of the scene. My spirit reached out and became one with the spirit of the sea and sky. I was one with the universe beyond. I seemed to become one with all life. This experience had a profound effect on me. It came to me often when I was alone with Nature. It swept over me as I looked out to the stars at night. It was a continuous inspiration. I felt that I was more than an individual. The life of all time was within me and about me . . . I have no sense of a personal God. My philosophy is founded on the experience I described. I cannot be other than a world citizen, identifying with all peoples.

Fenner Brockway

We are part of this natural universe and this natural world. We are part of the story of life on this planet. We can feel a real sense of belonging and connectedness in this story, and also a humility in the face of all the contingencies and chances that led to the survival of our species.

We're not the pinnacle of evolution but we do have special abilities that mean we have the power not only to understand but to transform the world around us.

We can manipulate our environment in ways and to a degree that no other animal can or has ever been able to do. We have the capacity to make tools and machines that help us to obtain food, to travel vast distances, and to survive in harsh environments. We have developed the ability to combat disease and to produce amazing architecture as well as great art and music. We are capable of all these things – but also of searing acts of destruction that place us and millions of other species at risk.

Our conscious appreciation of who we are and where we've come from brings with it a huge responsibility.

We are not just like every other animal: we are both incredibly powerful and aware of our impact.

Although denying that we have a special position in the natural world might seem becomingly modest in the eye of eternity, it might also be used as an excuse for evading our responsibilities. The fact is that no species has ever had such wholesale control over everything on earth, living or dead, as we now have. That lays upon us, whether we like it or not, an awesome responsibility. In our hands now lies not only our own future, but that of all other living creatures with whom we share the earth.

David Attenborough

The humanist approach has always been one of concern for other animals too.

Because of the word *humanist*, some people get the mistaken impression that this view of the world must be exclusively human-centred, not taking other animals into account.

Nothing could be further from the truth.

Because we are related to all living things and because we understand what it is to feel pain and pleasure ourselves, this gives us a moral connection to other animals that can feel.

> The question is not, 'Can they reason?' nor
> 'Can they talk?' but 'Can they suffer?'
> **Jeremy Bentham**

> We should be bound by the laws of humanity to
> give gentle usage to these creatures.
> **David Hume**

> The only justifiable stopping place for the
> expansion of altruism is the point at which
> all whose welfare can be affected by our actions
> are included within the circle of altruism.
> This means that all beings with the capacity
> to feel pleasure and pain should be included.
> **Peter Singer**

The World Organisation for Animal Health promotes 'five freedoms' for animals who are under human control. They are based on the assumption that we have a moral responsibility to other animals because they have needs and feelings:

1. **Freedom from hunger or thirst** by ready access to fresh water and a diet that maintains full health and vigour.

2. **Freedom from discomfort** by providing an appropriate environment including shelter and a comfortable resting area.

3. **Freedom from pain, injury or disease** by prevention or rapid diagnosis and treatment.

4. **Freedom to express normal behaviour** by providing sufficient space, proper facilities and company of the animal's own kind.

5. **Freedom from fear and distress** by ensuring conditions and treatment avoid mental suffering

We're facing enormous challenges this century. These include climate change and loss of biodiversity. The stakes are high: both for us and many other species on this planet.

While we try to sustain ourselves, in our billions, we must also seek to reduce our impact on the rest of the natural world, and take as many other species into the future with us as humanly possible.

Think about our descendants in a million years, or two. If the relics of our technology survive the ravages of time, how will those descendants look back on us? As inheritors of a power we were too naive to use well? Or as pioneers who made wise choices, nurturing the natural environment of which we are a part? What would you think if you were one of them?

Human nature is not a machine to be built after a model, and set to do exactly the work prescribed for it, but a tree, which requires to grow and develop itself on all sides, according to the tendency of the inward forces which make it a living thing.

John Stuart Mill

the unique you

Friendship with oneself is all-important
because without it one cannot be friends
with anyone else in the world.

Eleanor Roosevelt

The journey of life on this planet has been long and the generations of human beings before you, though shorter than the planet's lifespan, is still countless.

And here you are at the end of it. A product of all those millions of years of life in abundance, and of generation after generation of humans who survived against the odds.

There has never been another you and there never will be – and you are amazing!

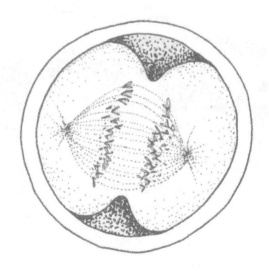

Our entire bodies and brains are made of a few dollars' worth of common elements: oxygen, hydrogen, nitrogen, carbon, enough calcium to whitewash a chicken coop, sufficient iron to make a two-inch nail, phosphorus to tip a good number of matches, enough sulphur to dust a flea-plagued dog, together with modest amounts of potassium, chlorine, magnesium and sodium.

Assemble them all in the right proportion, build the whole into an intricate interacting system, and the result is our feeling, thinking, striving, imagining, creative selves.

Such ordinary elements; such extraordinary results!

James Hemming

You are related to every animal on the planet, but you are different from other animals.

You don't just move through your life with events happening to you. You experience those events.

You can look back at them, think about them, and in your mind you give them meaning.

You can look forward and think about your future. You can make plans.

And you can choose to live this one life well.

Plants and animals reproduce themselves through sex, and many animals bring up their young, but it is love which makes sex and the family truly human, the personal love which binds parents and children, lovers and friends, the impersonal love which binds society and humanity.

Nicolas Walter

One of the things that you can think about is yourself.

You are unique because of your genes, because of the way in which you were raised, and because of all the experiences that you have had. You are unique because of your personality.

By working to know yourself, to understand why you do what you do, you can gradually improve yourself. This personal development is a lifelong pursuit – not just a one-off task but an ongoing process.

Every day brings the possibility of you knowing yourself better and living an even better life.

Be careful of your thoughts, for your thoughts become your words.

Be careful of your words, for your words become your actions.

Be careful of your actions, for your actions become your habits.

Be careful of your habits, for your habits become your character.

Be careful of your character, for your character becomes your destiny.

Traditional Chinese, often attributed to Lao Tzu

Be kind to yourself

As well as thinking about what you can improve in yourself, you also need to accept yourself for who you are. Practise self-compassion – accepting yourself with all your faults, frailties and foibles. It will be good for you and it will help you extend compassion to others.

You will become not just happier but more able to relate to others.

> One has to be friends with oneself before one is fit to be a friend. Nobody else is responsible for taking care of one's interests, satisfying one's needs and desires, fulfilling one's chosen possibilities, making a job of one's life. Doing the best for oneself can be the best one can do for others.
>
> **Harold Blackham**

Making a kinder you

Being kind is like a craft – you can get better at it through practice.

What can you do today to be a kinder person?

Try keeping a journal and writing down your kindnesses.

Reflect at the end of the week – have you made yourself a kinder person?

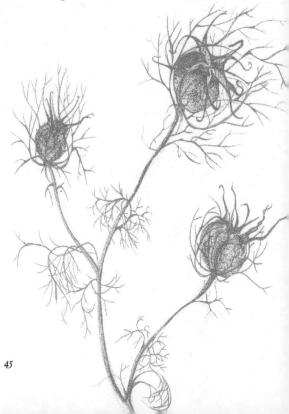

The importance of resilience

In 1940, the Dutch humanist Jaap van Praag went into hiding. He was ethnically Jewish and it was the only way to stay alive in the Nazi-occupied Netherlands. Remaining in hiding for the rest of the war, he thought about why so many people had been swept up by fascism by either becoming Nazis, or collaborating with Nazis.

For van Praag, the answer lay in resilience: if people could hold on to their integrity and continue to think independently, they would be less likely to give in to pressure to act against their values or better instincts – even when faced with adversity or opposition. People who possessed resilience in this way stood up to Nazis. People who lacked it, gave in.

Today, there is a whole school of psychology and counselling rooted in the humanist worldview and it is one of the most popular approaches to counselling in the world. Resilience is a key concept in it.

We can develop resilience in ourselves by reflecting on our values, thinking critically about the claims of others, and building healthy relationships with others.

Carl Rogers, a founder of humanistic psychology, wrote more on the fully functioning and resilient person:

> He is more able to experience all of his feelings, and is less afraid of any of his feelings; he is his own sifter of evidence, and is more open to evidence from all sources; he is completely engaged in the process of being and becoming himself, and thus discovers that he is soundly and realistically social; he lives more completely in this moment, but learns that this is the soundest living for all time. He is becoming a more fully functioning organism, and because of the awareness of himself which flows freely in and through his experience, he is becoming a more fully functioning person.

Each one of us is unique. A combination of genes that has never been seen before on planet Earth – a new 'experiment' in being human. And there is no archetypal human. You're just as perfect an example of *Homo sapiens* as the next person – as any person.

And the human species is the sum of its parts – all of that diversity.

Achieving one's full potential in skills, abilities, moral development and psychological well-being is to become a 'whole person'. Finding ways to encourage this fullness of being is an important part of the humanist agenda.

Jeaneane Fowler

This is what we do. We write and read, and we science and create and talk. We pass on knowledge and consider each other's minds. We try to be better than our primal urges, and we think about the options ahead, and make plans and choices about how to proceed. We struggle for existence and try to ease the struggles of others.

Adam Rutherford

diversity
and equality

All human beings are born free and equal in dignity and rights. They are endowed with reason and conscience and should act towards one another in a spirit of brotherhood.

Universal Declaration of Human Rights of the United Nations

Human beings like to feel part of a group

But sometimes, in order to achieve this, we put up barriers to protect the group identity and keep others out. If we're not careful, feeling like part of a group can lead to tribalism. All human groups – from families to nations – have some tendency to do this. Human beings also tend to be afraid, or at least suspicious, of anything or anyone new or different.

There may have been a survival advantage to this behaviour in our evolutionary past. It may be part of human nature, but that doesn't mean it's morally acceptable or that human beings can't progress beyond these primitive ways of thinking.

We know better now.

There are other aspects of human nature, including reason and empathy, that can help us to reject tribalism. We should nurture those better aspects of our nature.

As man advances in civilisation, and small tribes are united into larger communities, the simplest reason would tell each individual that he ought to extend his social instincts and sympathies to all the members of the same nation, though personally unknown to him. This point once reached, there is only an artificial barrier to prevent his sympathies extending to the men of all nations and races.

Charles Darwin

We have far more in common with each other than things that divide us.

Jo Cox

The radical idea of humanism is that every human being should be seen as having dignity and equal worth – simply by virtue of their humanity.

Once we understand that we are all part of the same species and the same long story, it is possible to feel a connection with all people, everywhere. We can imagine ourselves in their position and know that what happens to them, could happen to us.

All human beings should have a right to dignity and to our concern.

This feeling of empathy is strengthened by officially recognising and guaranteeing human rights. History has shown us that this is the best way to create more peaceful societies – for everyone.

I don't think I can improve on the formulation of the dramatist Terence: a former slave from Roman Africa, a Latin interpreter of Greek comedies, a writer from classical Europe who called himself Terence the African.

He once wrote, 'Homo sum, humani nihil a me alienum puto' or 'I am human, I think nothing human alien to me.'

Now there's an identity worth holding on to.

Kwame Anthony Appiah

Mutual respect is necessary if we want to live in a peaceful society.

Humanists think that our ability to use empathy and reason allows us to see how everyone's life would be improved if we were more tolerant of our differences.

There's good evidence that global society is making progress in this way, especially over the last century. There is a way to go, of course, and sometimes our own experiences or the media may make us think there is no progress at all. But over the last few generations, in many countries, we have seen people becoming less intolerant and more compassionate, with fewer people dying in violent conflicts.

Peace is more than just the absence of war.
Peace requires respect for the worth and dignity
of our fellow human beings, tolerance among
individuals and harmony within each person.
It also requires global justice in place of global
inequalities, not least the elimination of hunger
and thirst in a world that produces plenty.

Article 3, The Oslo Declaration on Peace,
2011 World Humanist Congress

It isn't enough to talk about peace. One must
believe in it. And it isn't enough to believe in it.
One must work at it.

Eleanor Roosevelt

Virtue can only flourish among equals

Mary Wollstonecraft was a remarkable woman. She lived in the eighteenth century, when women's lives were very restricted – but she was passionate about the idea of equality between women and men.

In her time, the whole structure of society was geared to favour and privilege men. Women couldn't receive a full education. They were banned from professions. They often had very little control at all over their own lives.

In 1792, Wollstonecraft published *A Vindication of the Rights of Women*, in which she argued that women were only ever inferior to men because they were treated unequally. If girls and boys were educated in an equal way, there would be no difference, she said. She had a vision for a better society, organised rationally, according to humanist principles.

Humanists today still believe in and fight for the human rights of women and equality of the sexes.

This is no simple reform. It really is a revolution. Sex and race, because they are easy, visible differences, have been the primary ways of organizing human beings into superior and inferior groups, and into the cheap labour on which this system still depends. We are talking about a society in which there will be no roles other than those chosen, or those earned. We are really talking about humanism.

Gloria Steinem

James Baldwin was a brilliant writer of fiction, and an activist for the human rights of black people and of gay people.

Baldwin – like many humanists concerned with equality – expressed rage at the injustice of discrimination. He was confident that it was possible, with people working together, to forge a better society.

> To be a negro in this country and to be relatively conscious is to be in a rage almost all the time.

> Love him and let him love you. Do you think anything else under heaven really matters?

> The world is before you and you need not take it or leave it as it was before you came in.

Like Baldwin, many humanists have campaigned against the racial prejudice and racism that exist in many societies. At the same time as struggling against racism, they have also often pointed out that, while 'race' exists as a social construct, it's biologically meaningless – human populations just can't be neatly divided up in this way.

> The myth of 'race' has created an enormous amount of human and social damage. In recent years it has taken a heavy toll in human lives and caused untold suffering. It still prevents the normal development of millions of human beings and deprives civilization of the effective co-operation of productive minds. The biological differences between ethnic groups should be disregarded from the standpoint of social acceptance and social action. The unity of mankind from both the biological and social viewpoint is the main thing.

Julian Huxley

> As far as genetics is concerned, race does not exist.

Adam Rutherford

The rights revolutions of the last century have given legal force to the idea of human equality.

In the twentieth century, people saw clearly – in the aftermath of horrific events such as world wars and genocides – that we needed to do better. Peace was something to strive for. And it was possible that human beings now had the power to prevent such horrors ever happening again on such a scale. We must dare to hope.

The Universal Declaration of Human Rights drafted in 1948 was a great affirmation of the humanist view that there are important moral values shared by all rational people, regardless of race, culture or religion – because they are based on our shared human nature and needs.

. . . recognition of the

inherent dignity and of the

equal and inalienable rights

of all members of the human

family is the foundation of

freedom, justice and peace

in the world . . .

Universal Declaration of Human Rights
of the United Nations

We all have human rights. Humanists believe that means we also have responsibilities.

The right to a private life is also the obligation to respect the privacy of others.

The right to freedom of expression and thought is also the obligation to be generous and make space for others to be heard.

The right to be treated with dignity is also the responsibility to respect the humanity and dignity of all other people.

You cannot hope to build a better world without improving the individuals. To that end, each of us must work for our own improvement and, at the same time, share a general responsibility for all humanity, our particular duty being to aid those to whom we think we can be most useful.

Marie Curie

Love is wise. Hatred is foolish. In this world, which is getting more and more closely interconnected, we have to learn to tolerate each other. We have to learn to put up with the fact that some people say things we don't like. We can only live together in that way. But if we are to live together, and not die together, we must learn a kind of charity and a kind of tolerance which is absolutely vital to the continuation of human life on this planet.

Bertrand Russell

The humanist vision of society is one which supports human flourishing – for all individuals.

This society would promote the freedom, prosperity, creativity and fulfilment of all individuals within it, whatever their class, colour, race, sex, gender, abilities or any other distinguishing feature.

In proportion to the development of his individuality, each person becomes more valuable to himself, and is therefore capable of being more valuable to others. There is a greater fullness of life about his own existence, and when there is more life in the units there is more in the mass which is composed of them.

John Stuart Mill

The individual is able to think, feel, strive, and work by himself; but he depends so much upon society – in his physical, intellectual, and emotional existence – that it is impossible to think of him, or to understand him, outside the framework of society. It is 'society' which provides man with food, clothing, a home, the tools of work, language, the forms of thought, and most of the content of thought; his life is made possible through the labour and the accomplishments of the many millions past and present who are all hidden behind the small word 'society'.

Albert Einstein

The story belongs not to any tribe, but to all of humanity . . . for it requires only the convictions that life is better than death, health is better than sickness, abundance is better than want, freedom is better than coercion, happiness is better than suffering, and knowledge is better than superstition and ignorance.

Steven Pinker

The increasing tendency towards seeing people in terms of one dominant 'identity' ('this is your duty as an American', 'you must commit these acts as a Muslim', or 'as a Chinese you should give priority to this national engagement') is not only an imposition of an external and arbitrary priority, but also the denial of an important liberty of a person who can decide on their respective loyalties to different groups (to all of which he or she belongs).

Amartya Sen

Believing in the essential unity of humanity doesn't mean we have to think everyone is or should be the same.

A humanist view of society is based firmly on the benefits of free thought, free expression, and the free exchange of ideas.

To be human is to think, to reason, to contend, and to relate to fellow human beings. Without a diversity of views to encounter and a diversity of people to engage with, we'd be lessened as individuals.

That principle of freedom of thought and expression should be extended to children too. No one – no matter how young – should ever be forced into following a religion or other tradition.

If the history of civilisation has any lesson to teach it is this: there is one supreme condition of mental and moral progress which it is completely within the power of man himself to secure, and that is perfect liberty of thought and discussion. The establishment of this liberty may be considered the most valuable achievement of modern civilisation, and as a condition of social progress it should be deemed fundamental. The considerations of permanent utility on which it rests must outweigh any calculations of present advantage which from time to time might be thought to demand its violation . . .

John Bagnell Bury

Children must be taught how to think, not what to think.

Margaret Mead

It is not by wearing down into uniformity all that is individual in themselves, but by cultivating it, and calling it forth, within the limits imposed by the rights and interests of others, that human beings become a noble and beautiful object of contemplation.

John Stuart Mill

being good

Is there one motto which we should follow our whole life?

Surely it is the rule of reciprocity: Don't do to others what you would not like yourself.

Confucius

In 2019, anthropologists at the University of Oxford published the results of their study tackling the question of morals – were morals different in different times and in different places? Or was morality essentially the same everywhere?

They had studied sixty groups, ranging from small tribes to large and complex societies. And they found seven universal rules – seven basic moral principles. These included helping others, dividing resources fairly, being brave and respecting the property of others.

As the lead author on the study, Oliver Scott Curry, said, 'All agree that cooperating, promoting the common good, is the right thing to do.'

Morality seems to have evolved to promote co-operation.

Mengzhi, also known as Mencius, was a philosopher and political adviser who was born about 2,400 years ago in China. He thought that human beings naturally had it in them to be good – and we just needed the right environment to draw that out of us.

All human beings have a constitution which suffers when it sees the suffering of others . . .

If people catch sight suddenly of a child about to fall into a well, they will all experience a feeling of alarm and distress . . .

Because we all have these feelings in ourselves, let us develop them, and the result will be like the blaze that is kindled from a small flame, or the spring in full spate that starts with a trickle. Let these feelings have a free rein, and they will be enough to give shelter and love to us all.

Mengzhi

Mengzhi was right!

In 2007, primatologists Megan van Wolkenten, Sarah Brosnan and Frans de Waal published the results of their study looking at whether monkeys understand fairness. In the study, pairs of monkeys performed simple tasks and were given food as a reward. But the researchers paid them unequally – giving one monkey a delicious grape and the other a piece of cucumber. Monkeys given the cucumber realised they'd been treated unfairly and were very obviously upset. Not only that, they were much less enthusiastic about performing the task again afterwards.

Scientists point out that social behaviour and instincts are rooted in our biology – and so are basic concepts like altruism and justice. We are, by nature, extremely social and cooperative.

But sociable behaviour can still be subverted by more negative, harmful tendencies. We all need the right environment around us to nurture our more positive instincts – to promote behaving well.

Why should I consider others? Myself, I think the only possible answer is the humanist one – because we are naturally social beings; we live in communities; and life in any community, from the family outwards, is much happier, and fuller, and richer if the members are friendly and cooperative than if they are hostile and resentful.

Margaret Knight

We have a natural head start in being good

Considering others is fundamental to our biology. But there's always room for improvement. We can get better at being good people by thinking about what being good really means, reflecting on the needs of others and ourselves.

Humanists don't believe in any supernatural source of commands or rules for being good. Instead, humanists hold that we need to think for ourselves about what sort of person we want to be and about the consequences of our actions.

Even people who say they're taking their morals from religious authority, sacred doctrines or holy books mostly have a very selective approach to this – carefully choosing parts that chime with what they already believe to be moral and ignoring other parts. So, they're not really learning moral lessons from scripture – rather, imposing their own morals on those archaic texts.

No moral system can rest solely on authority. It can never be sufficient justification for performing any action that someone wishes or commands it.

A.J. Ayer

A humanist is someone who always tries to do the right thing, even though no-one is watching.

Ricky Gervais

Accept responsibility

Your decisions matter and *you* are the one making them.

Even if you seek guidance from others, you still have to choose whether to accept that guidance.

We can't ever escape the fact that we have individual responsibility for deciding what to do – or what not to do.

We sometimes need to remind ourselves of this, especially in a world where things can often seem beyond our control.

It's a big responsibility. But it's also a reason to value and respect ourselves more – and to feel more free and more confident.

Ultimately the humanist view of morality is incredibly empowering. It means asserting that human beings have it within us to work out what is the right or wrong thing to do – using reason, empathy, compassion, and respect for the dignity of every person.

One ought always to ask

oneself what would happen

if everyone did as one

is doing.

Jean-Paul Sartre

One's philosophy is not

best expressed in words,

it is expressed in the

choices one makes.

Eleanor Roosevelt

What's right and what's wrong – and how do we know?

We're lucky that, over the last few thousand years, a lot of people have thought extremely hard about these questions – and their wisdom comes down to us. We don't just have to rely on our own ideas, or what our family or friends might say – we can learn from their ideas.

In all that's been written about what makes an action right or wrong, three main ideas have emerged: behaviour may be guided by rules, by consequences and by virtues.

Rules, consequences and virtues

There are broadly three different ways of thinking about what is right.

There are ethics based on **rules** about what is right and what is wrong. An action is considered wrong if it breaks a rule. The problems with this are clear – rules may be wrong and we may well question the motives of the rule-maker.

There are ethics founded on **consequences.** An action is thought to be wrong if it produces a harmful effect. We still have to decide what 'harm' means, but thinking about consequences seems a more rational and intelligent way to judge actions than just using rules.

Then there are ethics based on **virtues**. An action is right if it is the sort of thing a good person would do. We still have to decide what virtues a good person should have, but this offers a way of being moral through personal development and reflection.

When thinking about the right thing to do, humanists tend to prefer personal ethics based on virtues or consequences.

One 'rule' that is not really a rule at all is the **golden rule:** treat others as you would like to be treated yourself.

It's a common theme across societies and across time. The earliest recorded examples of it are in Egypt, 4,000 years ago, and in China, over 2,500 years ago.

But it can be worked out by anyone, anywhere, based on experience alone.

Almost every ethical tradition has this simple principle in some form, including almost all religions.

It works because it makes sense to individuals. You generally don't want to be lied to, victimised, stolen from, or harmed, so you can understand that others won't want this done to them either.

Of course, taking the golden rule at face value could encourage harmful acts: for example, someone who enjoys danger might try to justify putting other people in danger by saying that she'd welcome her own life being endangered by others.

'Do not do to others as you would that they should do to you. Their tastes may not be the same', the playwright George Bernard Shaw once joked.

Some humanists prefer the negative version of the golden rule: don't do anything to others that you wouldn't want done to you.

But that still means you're basing your behaviour on how *you* would like – or wouldn't like – to be treated.

Humanists think that the solution to this problem lies in thinking about other people's perspectives – simply asking other people what makes them happy and what makes them unhappy. Nobody wants anyone else to act in a way that affects us without taking into account our personal wishes and interests. So when we're thinking about the best thing to do, we need to use a combination of reason and empathy.

The golden rule relates to our specific likes and dislikes, but also plays out on a level above that: our *desire* to have our interests taken into account, our *wishes* fulfilled, and our *fears* avoided.

The philosopher Derek Parfit summed all this up by rewriting the golden rule:

> We ought to treat everyone as we would rationally be willing to be treated if we were going to be in all of those people's positions and would be relevantly like them.

It may lack the pithiness of the original but it works!

The power of empathy

One of the most important faculties we have to help us make better decisions, and to make ourselves better people, is empathy: our ability to think ourselves into other people's situations, to take their perspective.

How can you develop and nurture your own sense of empathy?

Talk to other people about their lives. Try to understand things from a different perspective.

In modern society, many of us live in a metaphorical echo chamber, where we only encounter beliefs and opinions similar to our own.

Living in a social bubble isn't good for our capacity for empathy. We should all do more to positively seek out people with different backgrounds, different experiences and different views from our own.

If we ever hope to be compassionate, we have to be able to think about a situation from someone else's perspective. We need to understand what it feels like to suffer injustice or discrimination, to be exploited or betrayed.

One of the best ways to develop empathy is to read stories. Whether historical or fictional, stories about particular individuals enable us to experience different lives.

When you read stories, think about the characters. Why do they do what they do? How have their own experiences shaped their actions? What would you do in their position?

A picture of human life such as a great artist can give, surprises even the trivial and selfish into that attention to what is apart from themselves, which may be called the raw material of moral sentiment . . . Art is the nearest thing to life; it is a mode of amplifying experience and extending our contact with our fellow-men beyond the grounds of our personal lot.

George Eliot

Empathy can get us a long way, but it's not enough on its own.

We need to combine empathy with reason.

We need to consider carefully the particular situation and the effects of our choices on the happiness or suffering of the people concerned – and the wider community. We need to do the same when we're thinking about how we affect other sentient animals, as well.

We need to weigh up the evidence, the probable consequences of the action – or of not acting – and the rights and wishes of those involved. That will help us find the kindest course of action, or the option that will do the least harm.

Actions are right in proportion
as they tend to promote
happiness, wrong as they
tend to produce the reverse
of happiness.

John Stuart Mill

Each moral choice is different

Every time we have to make a difficult moral choice, there will be something new and different about it. So applying the same rule every time is not going to work.

It doesn't mean our values have changed. It's more that the situations in which we apply them are different – and so we make different choices in practice.

This requires careful thought. Sometimes, we might find we've settled into ways of thinking that mean we're applying rules, even if those are our own rules. We need to challenge ourselves – not just acting on what seems like instinct or intuition but going back to thinking carefully about consequences and virtues again.

I've vacillated throughout my life thinking I was utilitarian because I do want the greater good. [Utilitarians] believe that you have to do something for the greater good, even if it's, 'I've got to push you off the cliff to save everyone in this room.' A utilitarian would say, 'Got to do it.'

A Kantian would say, 'Do the right thing in the moment, which is even if everyone else has to die, I have to save you. I will not push you off the cliff.' And I find both of those really compelling arguments.

. . . the ability to vacillate between either of those two theories . . . I think that's where I land.

Kristen Bell

Believing you have to work things out for yourself is not the same as saying that moral principles are simply matters of personal preference:

Most of us want to get on well with those around us. We want to live in peace with others rather than in a climate of hostility and anger. We know that love enriches our lives, and that hatred diminishes us. Most of us value cooperation with others, and the satisfaction we get from applying our shared energies to a common task.

To cooperate with one another, we need to be able to rely on one another and trust one another. That is why we need the values of honesty, of loyalty, of being reliable, and keeping our promises and agreements. When we cooperate, we need also the value of fairness. We need to feel that everyone is doing their fair share of the work, and getting a fair share of the rewards and benefits. We are reluctant to cooperate if we feel that we are being used and exploited.

If we are to live and work with others, we will also need to recognise and live with our differences. We have different tastes and preferences. To some extent we espouse different ways of life. So we need values of respect and tolerance for one another. We value freedom to live our own lives. But we also recognise that if we are to live cooperatively with one another we have to accept limits to that freedom, at the point where it infringes the freedom of others. We may want to put this in the language of 'rights', and the most basic right is perhaps the right to mutual respect.

We won't all come up with the same list of values. But we seem already to have a plausible list of values which many people would accept – kindness, consideration, peace, love, cooperation, honesty, loyalty, fairness, mutual respect and tolerance. The list may even seem obvious. If it does, that is all to the good, for it bears out one of the most basic tenets of humanism – that there are shared human values.

Richard Norman

Most of the social and political evils of the world arise through absence of sympathy and presence of hatred, envy, or fear . . . Every kind of hostile action or feeling provokes a reaction by which it is increased and so generates a progeny of violence and injustice which has a terrible vitality. This can only be met by cultivating in ourselves and attempting to generate in the young feelings of friendliness rather than hostility, of well-wishing rather than malevolence, and of co-operation rather than competition . . .

If I am asked 'Why do you believe this?' I should not appeal to any supernatural authority, but only to the general wish for happiness. A world full of hate is a world full of sorrow. From the point of view of worldly wisdom, hostile feeling and limitation of sympathy are folly. Their fruits are war, death, oppression, and torture, not only for their original victims but, in the long run, also for their perpetrators or their descendants. Whereas if we could all learn to love our neighbours, the world would quickly become a paradise for us all.

Bertrand Russell

thinking clearly

Humanists do not claim to know, we just ask you to be very wary of those who do claim to know. Who told them? What does their knowledge mean? Why should you trust them? Above all, don't take my word for it either. Don't take anybody's word for it. Find out for yourselves.

Stephen Fry

Human beings are not always good at accepting the truth.

We fool ourselves into thinking that things are right or true for all sorts of reasons. Maybe because it is fashionable to think something, or because someone we trust has told us, or because it's something we've believed for a long time. We *want* to believe it – even if it's not true.

There's a name for this sort of impediment to clear thinking: cognitive bias.

Cognitive biases work as shortcuts in your thinking that allow you to come to conclusions more quickly. They can be useful rules of thumb, saving you time in making decisions by simplifying your perception of situations.

But cognitive biases can also lead you to jump to the wrong conclusion – and make bad choices.

Two common cognitive biases to recognise – and to try to avoid.

Anchoring bias – We tend to focus far too much on the first thing we learn about a new topic, and then we judge any new information relative to the information we already have in hand. For example, if we go into a shop and see that a loaf of bread costs £3, and then go to another shop where a loaf is £2, it seems cheap. But it may be that a loaf costs only £1 in all the other shops on the street. Our opinion has been led by the first thing we saw.

Confirmation bias – We tend to look more actively for information that confirms something we already believe, and discount information that counters what we already believe. We also tend to think that evidence which supports our existing views is better quality, even if it isn't. And we're more likely to remember information that agrees with us, and forget information that doesn't.

There are many more cognitive biases (hundreds, in fact) that psychologists have identified. The more you can learn about and try to avoid them, the clearer your own thinking will be . . .

How can we know what is true and what is real?

We need to look for good reasons and for evidence.

Children are always asking, 'Why?'

Although this is sometimes really annoying, they've got entirely the right idea!

Asking for explanations and for evidence is *never* a bad thing.

A wise man proportions his

belief to the evidence.

David Hume

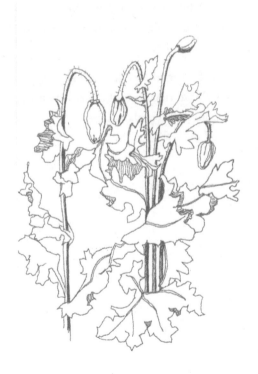

Unreliable evidence

We can reject certain possible sources of knowledge – because we know they don't work or are improbable.

For example, we can reject the idea that knowledge can come from supernatural revelation, prophetic visions or divinely inspired books.

These alleged sources of knowledge are not only serially unreliable and internally inconsistent, there are no good explanations or reasons for how they *could* ever work.

When anyone tells me, that he saw a dead man restored to life, I immediately [wonder] whether it be more probable that this person should either deceive or be deceived, or that the fact . . . should really have happened.

David Hume

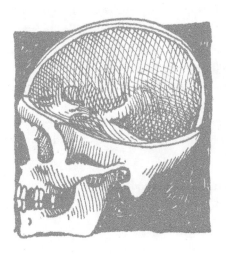

Knowledge we can rely on

Out of all the various methods that people have tried to use to find out how the world works, observation, experimentation and testing theories against evidence have the best track record.

In practice, this is how we understand the world around us every day – observing cause and effect. Science takes this further and helps us combat our preconceptions, uncovering facts which are not immediately obvious.

> Science is simply common sense at its best, that is, rigidly accurate in observation, and merciless to fallacy in logic.
>
> **Thomas Henry Huxley**

Sights, sounds, glimpses, smells and touches all provide reasons for beliefs. If John comes in and gets a good doggy whiff, he acquires a reason for believing that Rover is in the house. If Mary looks in the fridge and sees the butter, she acquires a reason for believing that there is butter in the fridge. If John tries and tries but cannot clear the bar, he learns that he cannot jump six feet. In other words, it is the whole person's interaction with the whole surround that gives birth to reasons.

Simon Blackburn

Truth isn't relative

Truth may be difficult to discern, but that doesn't mean it's not real.

Just as you shouldn't believe those who say that truth can come from revelations or visions or holy books, you shouldn't believe those who say that there is no such thing as truth at all, or that we can all have our 'own truths'.

Be sceptical – question everything

This applies even to your own memories and what you find yourself saying. It's hard to understand our own instincts and behaviours, and memory plays tricks on us more often than we think. Every time we recall a memory we change it in some way, and it may not even have been that accurate in the first place.

We must constantly check the results of our reasoning process against the facts, and see if they fit. If they don't fit, we must respect the facts, and conclude that our reasoning was mistaken.

J.B.S. Haldane

Falsehood is so easy, truth so difficult. The pencil is conscious of a delightful facility in drawing a griffin – the longer the claws, and the larger the wings, the better; but that marvellous facility which we mistook for genius is apt to forsake us when we want to draw a real unexaggerated lion.

Examine your words well, and you will find that even when you have no motive to be false, it is a very hard thing to say the exact truth, even about your own immediate feelings – much harder than to say something fine about them which is not the exact truth.

George Eliot

There is no immemorial tradition, no revelation, no authority, no privileged knowledge (first principles, intuitions, axioms) which is beyond question . . . There is only experience to be interpreted in the light of further experience, the sole source of all standards of reason and value, for ever open to question. This radical assumption is itself, of course, open to question, and stands only in so far as it is upheld by experience.

Harold Blackham

It might be said that 'distrust thy father and mother' is the first commandment with promise. It should be a part of education to explain to children as soon as they are old enough to understand, when it is reasonable, and when it is not, to accept what they are told on authority.

John Bagnell Bury

Some people really are lying to you

You can't always tell today when something is a lie. Especially in the age of unmoderated social media, something designed to deceive you can be so clever and complete-looking that you will not see that it is false. But there are ways you can examine an argument to see whether it is truthful or not.

Logical fallacies are often used by people trying to deceive us or persuade us of things that are not true. But it's good to look out for them in all arguments you encounter, as the person making the argument may not be intending to deceive – they may themselves believe what they're telling you – and just be wrong.

Three common logical fallacies to recognise (and call out)

False cause arguments – This is when someone argues that because B happens after A (or at the same time as A), then A must have caused B. For example, Daniel says that on Tuesday he dyed his hair green and on Wednesday Robert agreed to marry him, therefore it was his green hair that did the trick.

Straw man arguments – This is when you misrepresent someone else's argument to make it easier to attack. For example, Jane says that she thinks the positive effects of private involvement in the state health service have been underestimated. Donald replies that he can't believe that Jane wants to privatise the health service and leave poor people to die on the street.

False dichotomy – This is when someone says, 'Either A or B is true and if B isn't, then A is', but in fact there are other possibilities. For example, Clive says that either Jesus was the true son of god or he was a fictional character.

Of course, a claim being made by someone using logical fallacies may be true (just badly argued). Jesus may indeed have been a fictional character, Jane may want poor people to die on the street, and Robert may have got engaged to Daniel because of his green hair. But these things are not proven by the arguments above.

Equally, an argument that contains no logical fallacies may still be false – for example, if the information it is based on is incorrect.

Bertrand Russell's *A Liberal Decalogue* was written in the 1950s as a guide to critical thinking in an age when politics and society were littered with many popular fallacies. Russell advised:

1. Do not feel absolutely certain of anything.

2. Do not think it worthwhile to proceed by concealing evidence, for the evidence is sure to come to light.

3. Never try to discourage thinking, for you are sure to succeed.

4. When you meet with opposition, even if it should be from your husband or your children, endeavour to overcome it by argument and not by authority, for a victory dependent upon authority is unreal and illusory.

5. Have no respect for the authority of others, for there are always contrary authorities to be found.

6 Do not use power to suppress opinions you think pernicious, for if you do the opinions will suppress you.

7. Do not fear to be eccentric in opinion, for every opinion now accepted was once eccentric.

8. Find more pleasure in intelligent dissent than in passive agreement, for, if you value intelligence as you should, the former implies a deeper agreement than the latter.

9. Be scrupulously truthful, even if the truth is inconvenient, for it is more inconvenient when you try to conceal it.

10. Do not feel envious of the happiness of those who live in a fool's paradise, for only a fool will think that it is happiness.

Don't think it's bad to change your mind – it can be a virtue.

Good scientists and historians are always prepared to change their opinions if new evidence contradicts them. They put forward revised theories, also to be tested. That's how our understanding of the world has increased.

The reason we know that many theories are true is because they have passed such tests. And it is not just academics who apply this method – we can all use it in our daily lives to improve our understanding and decide what is true.

If you're not lucky enough to have someone to argue against you, you can do it yourself!

Think about what someone who would disagree with you would think – how would they argue the case? Try to frame their case in the best way possible, then consider your reaction. This technique is known as making a 'steel man' argument. Instead of making a 'straw man' of an argument you disagree with, you're doing the opposite.

When my information changes, I change my mind.
What do you do?

Attributed to John Maynard Keynes

The personal virtues which humanism cherishes are
intelligence, amenity, and tolerance; the particular
courage it asks for is that which is exercised
in the support of these virtues. The qualities of
intelligence which it chiefly prizes are modulation
and flexibility.

Lionel Trilling

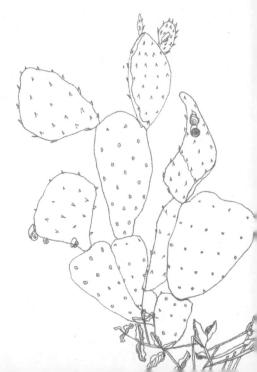

Reality check

There *is* such a thing as truth and you are more likely to know what is true if you are thinking more clearly.

Thinking critically – not just about what others are saying but about your own beliefs too – means you'll be more aware of reality. And the more aware of reality you are, the more of an honest and authentic life you can live.

You'll have a better chance of improving not just your own life, but the lives of others, your society, and our world – if you think clearly and face reality with courage.

Beliefs are of two types, those we can verify and articulate, and those we simply accept without verification and which we more vaguely express. The more of the former we have, the more developed we are as human beings.

Jeaneane Fowler

Not everything that is faced can be changed but nothing can be changed until it is faced.

James Baldwin

science and progress

Nothing in life is to be feared.
It is only to be understood.

Marie Curie

Sometimes when we look around at the world, we can get depressed. But in fact, this is one of the best – if not *the* best – times to have ever been born.

Some people hark back to the idea of a lost 'golden age' when human beings may have been poorer and life shorter, but were spiritually richer. Now, they say, we are materially better off but spiritually impoverished.

But do we really believe that it is preferable – and somehow spiritually enriching – to be poor, hungry, starving, ignorant, disease-ridden and dying young? Surely not.

Those who are always praising the past
and especially the time of faith as best
ought to go and live in the Middle Ages
and be burnt at the stake as witches and sages.

Stevie Smith

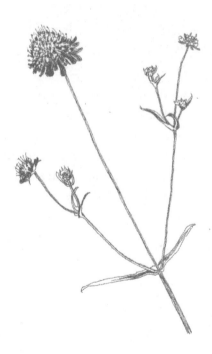

Human progress is real

Some people deny the idea of progress. But it is very strange to look back into history and prehistory – to see how our understanding of the world has increased, how humans are now able to live longer and healthier lives, how superstition has given way to science, how culture has flourished – and not see that as progress.

Much of this progress has been down to the advance of science as a way of understanding the world and of developing technologies to improve our lives. There are certainly big challenges facing us now, but we don't need to resign ourselves to despair or ignorance. Instead, we can afford to be optimistic about the potential to improve lives – by human effort.

The notion that a person shall judge for themselves what they are told, sifting the evidence and weighing the conclusions, is of course implicit in the outlook of science.

But it begins before that as a positive and active constituent of humanism. For evidently the notion implies not only that man is free to judge, but that he is able to judge.

This is an assertion of confidence.

Jacob Bronowski

Marie Curie was a woman ahead of her time.

Maria Sklodowska was born in 1867, in Russian-occupied Poland. As a woman, she was officially excluded from higher education – but she still managed to study science. Aged twenty-four, she moved to Paris where she continued her studies and met the scientist Pierre Curie – whom she would marry.

She investigated uranium and radioactivity, working in a converted shed. In 1898, she and Pierre announced the discovery of two new elements to the world: polonium and radium. In 1903, they were both invited to the Royal Institution in London to talk about their discoveries – but only Pierre, as a man, was allowed to speak.

Marie would go on to win two Nobel prizes for her work in both physics and chemistry.

The dangers of radium and radioactivity were only properly understood much later. Marie Curie herself died from anaemia thought to have been brought on by years of exposure to radioactivity.

Marie Curie was immensely influential, and her life has been an inspiration for many humanists, who have admired her dedication to truth and her relentless curiosity. Her discoveries led to major advances in physics, demonstrating that atoms were divisible. Radioactivity would have far-reaching applications, including treating cancer.

Marie Curie is remembered as an iconic pioneer – and a woman who overcame many social barriers to become a world-class scientist.

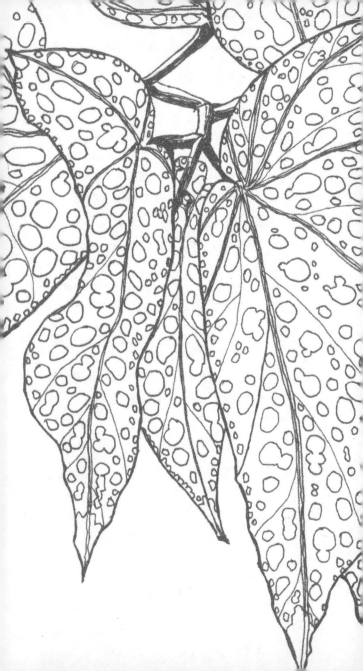

Isn't it a noble, an enlightened way of spending our brief time in the sun, to work at understanding the universe and how we have come to wake up in it? This is how I answer when I am asked – as I am surprisingly often – why I bother to get up in the mornings. To put it the other way round, isn't it sad to go to your grave without wondering why you were born? Who, with such a thought, would not spring from bed eager to resume discovering the world and rejoicing to be part of it?

Richard Dawkins

Science values truth and looks for disagreement and debate to approach the truth more closely. Scientists look at evidence and suggest hypotheses – explanations for the phenomena they're observing. But then – crucially – they test those hypotheses against the evidence again.

Over time, the explanations get better and better. Science allows us to reach back in time, to discover how our universe came into being, how life evolved on earth, and to understand the fabric of reality in wonderful detail – from atoms to solar systems. It also underpins all our technology, from mobile phones to medicine, space rockets to satellite navigation, Wi-Fi to wind turbines.

I may be wrong and you may be right and, by an effort, we may get nearer the truth.

Karl Popper

Humanists embrace science – as our best tool for understanding how the world works, for making human lives better, and for understanding how best to nurture the rest of life on this planet.

> To put it most simply, humanists believe that human beings produced the progressive advance of human society and also the ills that plague it. They believe that if the ills are to be alleviated, it is humanity that will have to do the job.
>
> **Isaac Asimov**

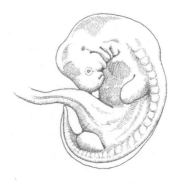

'But science has had its chance to make us good – and look at the world! It's failed!' some people say.

Biologist and writer Sir Peter Medawar mused on this back in 1959, when people were questioning whether science really was helping society to make progress. He thought we often focused too much on the negatives and forgot how much better our lives had become, through the application of science and technology:

> We wring our hands over the miscarriages of technology and take its benefactions for granted. We are dismayed by air pollution but not proportionately cheered up by, say, the virtual abolition of poliomyelitis.

Medawar also thought that we shouldn't be dismayed that we hadn't achieved all our ambitions *yet*. He thought that we should be realistic about progress – some had been made, but there was still much further to go – and that we could dare to be optimistic about the future.

> We are still beginners, and for that reason may hope to improve. To deride the hope of progress, is the last word in poverty of spirit and meanness of mind.

That theme was echoed by physician and writer Alexander Comfort:

> When we hear it said that science has already failed to make us good, I always want to draw attention to the time-scale of things. There have been recognizable men for about a million years. There have been fairly highly developed human societies (I stand to be corrected on this) for about 12,000 years.
>
> If we date the description of the scientific method from Bacon, then it hås been in existence for 300 years. It has been seriously applied to medicine and natural sciences for about 200 years with the results we know. It has been applied to human social behaviour for eighty to a hundred years. In that time it has already produced a greater revolution both in human awareness and, I think it is true to say, in human ethics, than religion has produced in several centuries – and its rate of progress in all these fields tends to be exponential; it is likely to go faster the farther it moves.

Alexander Comfort was also the author of *The Joy of Sex*, published in 1972, the first popular book to treat sex as something to be enjoyed. This is also part of human progress: removing the taboos attached to natural and enjoyable parts of life.

If religion is the opiate of the people, tradition is
an even more sinister analgesic, simply because it
rarely appears sinister. If religion is a tight band,
a throbbing vein, and a needle, tradition is a far
homelier concoction: poppy seeds ground into tea;
a sweet cocoa drink laced with cocaine; the kind
of thing your grandmother might have made.

Zadie Smith

The way that human societies have become more enlightened is through reason, through realising fellow feeling, prizing helping others and aspiring to build better futures for all.

William Beveridge was a rare thing among the educated British elite in the nineteenth century – a second-generation humanist, following his father. In 1942 he wrote the report which invented the welfare state to alleviate poverty and create social justice.

> The object of government in peace and in war is not the glory of rulers or of races, but the happiness of the common man.

John Boyd Orr was a Scottish humanist who became the first director-general of the UN Food and Agriculture Organization in 1945. He dedicated his life to promoting the use of science to end hunger in the world and won the Nobel Peace Prize for his efforts in 1949.

> Our civilisation has evolved through the continuous adjustment of society to the stimulus of new knowledge.

Brock Chisholm was a Canadian humanist who was the first director-general of the World Health Organization, from 1948 to 1953. He dedicated his life to the idea of sustainable development and an improved world, especially through education.

> Unless we are very careful, very careful indeed, and very conscientious, there is still great danger that our children may turn out to be the same kind of people we are.

Jennie Lee and her husband **Aneurin Bevan** were humanist MPs who between them created two great progressive institutions in the UK. Lee created the Open University (opening in 1969), dedicated to offering university education to those denied the opportunity in previous generations. Bevan was responsible for creating the National Health Service in 1948 to provide free healthcare to all regardless of wealth.

> No society can legitimately call itself civilised if a sick person is denied medical aid because of lack of means.

Amartya Sen is an Indian humanist who has worked in the fields of both philosophy and economics, and pioneered an approach to development that puts human beings at the centre rather than national economic development.

> Human development, as an approach, is concerned with what I take to be the basic development idea: namely, advancing the richness of human life, rather than the richness of the economy in which human beings live, which is only a part of it.

Now, our understanding of the world is better because of physical science. Our understanding of ourselves is better because of biological science. We live longer, and we feed ourselves better, and 'we' here includes not only people in first world countries, but countless people in the third world.

We look after the environment better, and in time we will manage our own numbers better. Outside the theocracies of the East more people have more freedoms and enjoy more education, more opportunities and may even have more rights than ever before.

We owe this progress entirely to the culture forged, in the West, by Bacon and Locke, Hume and Voltaire, Newton and Darwin.

Humanism is the belief that humanity need not be ashamed of itself, and these are its great examples.

They show us that we need not regard knowledge as impious, or ignorance as desirable, and we need not see blind faith as anything other than blind.

Simon Blackburn

There is no harmony between religion and science. When science was a child, religion sought to strangle it in the cradle.

Now that science has attained its youth, and superstition is in its dotage, the trembling, palsied wreck says to the athlete: 'Let us be friends.'

It reminds me of the bargain the cock wished to make with the horse: 'Let us agree not to step on each other's feet.'

Robert G. Ingersoll

'A fire-breathing dragon lives in my garage'

Suppose I seriously make such an assertion to you. Surely you'd want to check it out, see for yourself. There have been innumerable stories of dragons over the centuries, but no real evidence. What an opportunity!

'Show me,' you say. I lead you to my garage. You look inside and see a ladder, empty paint cans, an old tricycle – but no dragon.

'Where's the dragon?' you ask.

'Oh, she's right here,' I reply, waving vaguely. 'I neglected to mention that she's an invisible dragon.'

You propose spreading flour on the floor of the garage to capture the dragon's footprints.

'Good idea,' I say, 'but this dragon floats in the air.'

Then you'll use an infrared sensor to detect the invisible fire.

'Good idea, but the invisible fire is also heatless.'

You'll spray-paint the dragon and make her visible.

'Good idea, but she's an incorporeal dragon and the paint won't stick.'

And so on. I counter every physical test you propose with a special explanation of why it won't work.

Now, what's the difference between an invisible, incorporeal, floating dragon who spits heatless fire and no dragon at all?

Carl Sagan

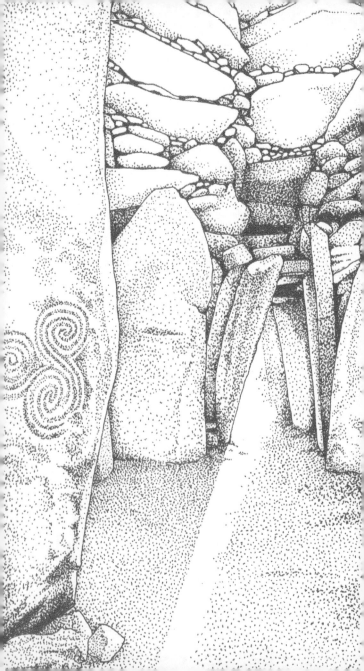

religion and faith

When I ceased to accept the teachings of my youth, it was not so much a process of giving up beliefs, as of discovering that I had never really believed.

Leslie Stephen

Human societies have had many gods and goddesses. We know of thousands of them, from Zeus, Yemoja and Shangdi to Juno, Ganesha and the singular gods of the Bible or Quran. And there are no doubt thousands more of them, no trace or memory of which have survived.

Where did all these gods come from? To humanists, they all seem to be the products of human imagination and culture. It's possible to trace the development of such myths and beliefs through time. And it's interesting that old gods look so much like the human beings that made them.

Desert dwellers invented harsh and dry austere gods. Farmers invented gods of harvest and plenty. It's also true of individuals today: there are no liberals who believe in a conservative god, or vice versa. Kind people believe in kind gods, and cruel people in cruel ones.

If cattle, horses, and lions had
hands and could paint and
make art just like humans can,
then horses would make horse-
shaped gods and cattle would
make cow-shaped ones.

Xenophanes

Why did more people in the past believe in gods?

People knew much less about how the natural world worked – and were at the mercy of frightening natural events such as lightning, earthquakes or rainstorms.

They looked for explanations in terms that they could understand and imagined supernatural beings (really like super-humans) who were responsible for the apparently meaningless events in the natural world. These superbeings could sometimes be appeased and that helped to give the illusion of control.

Modern neuroscientists suggest that this belief would have been psychologically healthy at the time – it would have helped bring a sense of meaning and relieve dread.

It was Fear that first made Gods in this world.

Publius Papinius Statius

Humans uniquely know that they have been born
. . . and that they will die. We understand that we,
as individuals, had a beginning, and that we will
not endure for ever.

And I suspect that all of religion is, at its roots, at
its foundations, concerned with giving us solace in
the face of this frankly unimaginable – but at the
same time, incontestable and unavoidable – fact.

Alice Roberts

Humanists are with those who do not believe there are any gods.

Religious people believe in one, or a few gods, and reject all the others. Humanists just go one step further, rejecting belief in all of them.

Humanists may be atheist or agnostic.

Some may believe strongly that there are *definitely* no gods, based on the fact they've just noted that all gods everywhere look so suspiciously like the people who worshipped them.

Some may think only that there are *probably* no gods and since they can't be sure, then it doesn't make sense to believe in any one of them.

Others think that the topic is just a pointless or irrelevant one – as it's perfectly possible to live your life well and with meaning without wasting time on wondering whether invisible, undetectable gods exist.

I can't know whether the gods exist or not, nor what they are like if they do. Two things in particular prevent any certain knowledge – the topic is obscure and life is short.

Protagoras

It's all a matter of ideas, and God is just one idea I don't accept. It's not important.
I don't even think about it. It's just that I get so tired of Him getting credit for all the things the human race achieves through its own stubborn effort.

Lorraine Hansberry

Religious explanations

Religions are human inventions. All the stories and legends, all the moral rules and visions, all the art and the temples and the music. They are all the work of human beings and our minds and hard work.

We might appreciate the art and architecture, music and literature that has emerged in religious contexts through time. But as ways of understanding the reality of the material universe, religious ideas themselves are out of date.

The natural world is wonderful enough, without imagining a supernatural dimension to it.

It is far better to grasp the
universe as it really is than to
persist in delusion, however
satisfying and reassuring.

Carl Sagan

Only animals live entirely in the Here and Now. Only nature knows neither memory nor history. But man – let me offer you a definition – is the storytelling animal. Wherever he goes he wants to leave behind not a chaotic wake, not an empty space, but the comforting marker-buoys and trail-signs of stories. He has to go on telling stories. He has to keep on making them up. As long as there's a story, it's all right.

Graham Swift

Stories with supernatural characters, for some people, are what give meaning and significance to this world. But for humanists, these types of story are ultimately empty – because they are imaginary.

> Isn't it enough to see that a garden is beautiful without having to believe that there are fairies at the bottom of it too?

Douglas Adams

> I maintain that faith in this world is perfectly possible without faith in another.

Rosalind Franklin

> I can stand at the beach's edge with the most devout Christian, Jew, Buddhist . . . and weep with the beauty of all this universe and be moved by all of humanity – all the billions of people who have lived before us, who have loved and hurt.

Diana Nyad

Many humanists never had religion in their lives. Others had religious upbringings which left them unsatisfied.

Religions were held out to them as providing answers, but they didn't.

Perhaps they found that religions didn't answer their questions about reality and the world around them. It doesn't make sense, for example, that any good god deserving of worship would allow all the suffering we see in the world.

Perhaps they found the religion unethical – for example, in the way it treated women, or gay people, or children, or people of different beliefs, or non-human animals.

Perhaps they found religions just didn't provide the meaning they claimed to give, in a world so different from the world in which they were invented.

Learning about the nature of space and time or the structure of atoms fills me with awe and wonder; it makes me want to learn more. I see a beauty in the laws of nature that can be explained by science. For me, to simply say 'It is so wonderful, it must have been designed by a Creator' is to avoid the issue. After all, who then designed the Creator?

Jim Al-Khalili

People sometimes say to me, 'Why don't you admit that the hummingbird, the butterfly, the Bird of Paradise are proof of the wonderful things produced by Creation?' And I always say, well, when you say that, you've also got to think of a little boy sitting on a river bank, like here, in West Africa, that's got a little worm, a living organism, in his eye and boring through the eyeball and is slowly turning him blind. The Creator God that you believe in, presumably, also made that little worm.

David Attenborough

Often there is a seeming truce between the humanist and the religious believer, but in fact their attitudes cannot be reconciled: one must choose between this world and the next. And the enormous majority of human beings, if they understood the issue, would choose this world. They do make that choice when they continue working, breeding, and dying instead of crippling their faculties in the hope of obtaining a new lease of existence elsewhere.

George Orwell

Some humanists don't feel very strongly about the fact that people believe things that aren't true.

It seems to me that organized creeds are collections of words around a wish. I feel no need for such. However, I would not, by word or deed, attempt to deprive another of the consolation it affords. It is simply not for me. Somebody else may have my rapturous glance at the archangels. The springing of the yellow line of morning out of the misty deep of dawn is glory enough for me.

Zora Neale Hurston

I find the religious presentation of sin and virtue uncongenial. I have come to the conclusion, however, after much voluntary and public work in the field of race relations, that the contribution of the major religions to our culture and their current importance to very many individuals means that non-religious people should respect and value religious affinity.

Janet Whitaker

Other humanists have a different reaction to religion . . .

I regard religion with fear and suspicion. It's not enough to say I don't believe in God. I regard religion as distressing. I'm offended by things said in the Bible and Koran.

Emma Thompson

I like, or anyhow tolerate, most religions so long as they are weak . . . But I dread them all, without exception, when they become powerful.

E.M. Forster

If the concept of God has any validity or any use, it can only be to make us larger, freer, and more loving. If God cannot do this, then it is time we got rid of Him.

James Baldwin

The conflict between humanists and religionists has always been one between the torch of enlightenment and the chains of enslavement.

Wole Soyinka

Ultimately humanists believe in freedom of belief for all and in working with others of different beliefs.

> All around the world and at all times, it is freedom of thought and freedom of expression that have proved the most essential conditions for human flourishing . . .
>
> The best response to the expression of a view we disagree with is to reply to it. Violence and censorship are never legitimate responses.
>
> **Oxford Declaration on Freedom of Thought and Expression, the 2014 World Humanist Congress of Humanists International**

thinking about death

We have two lives, and the second begins
when we realize we only have one.

Attributed to Confucius

Close your eyes and think back over your life so far. What is your earliest memory? Perhaps you can just about remember an early birthday, a favourite toy, or an early playmate. Try to think back further, as far as you can.

Try to think about what it was like before you were born.

If that is too much of a stretch, think about how it feels when you're asleep. Not the moments when you're half-awake or dreaming. Think about how you feel during dreamless sleep.

. . .

The point, of course, is that you *can't* remember either of these things – neither dreamless sleep nor the years before your birth.

Look back on the eternity that passed before
we were born and consider how it counts as
absolutely nothing to us. This is a mirror, held up
for us by Nature, that shows how it will be after
we are dead. Is there anything frightening in this
sight? Anything depressing? Anything that is not
more restful than the deepest of sleeps?

Lucretius

We are such stuff
As dreams are made on; and our little life
Is rounded with a sleep.

William Shakespeare

The mind grows like the body; like the body,
it inherits characteristics from both parents; it is
affected by diseases of the body and by drugs;
it is intimately connected with the brain. There is
no scientific reason to suppose that after death
the mind acquires an independence of the brain
which it never had in life.

Bertrand Russell

Once upon a time, we did not understand that thinking happened in our brains. People believed it was possible that the part of us that thought, and looked out at the world, was separate from our body. Now we know that is not so.

Our minds are simply what our brain *does*. The brain – and mind – are part of our body. Our personality matures and changes just as our body grows and changes. If someone's brain is damaged by injury or age, they change in themselves. You aren't living in your body – you *are* your body. Body and mind are inseparable.

Why should we think we can live outside of time and matter? No other part of nature can. The fact that we will end is just that – an inescapable fact.

Humanists accept the fact that life ends at death.

Fear of death is a perfectly natural emotion. Humanists believe we should acknowledge that our death represents the end of our existence and have the opportunity to articulate and discuss our feelings about that fact.

However, death is a natural part of life and many humanists will argue that we can find ways, and can support each other, to cope with our fears about death: they believe that human beings are psychologically strong enough to do this.

All of us will die, and most of us will suffer before we do so. 'The last act is bloody, however fine the rest of the play may be,' said Pascal. Raging against the dying of the light may be good art, but is bad advice. 'Why me?' may be a natural question, but it prompts a natural answer: 'Why not?' Religion may promise life everlasting, but we should grow up and accept that life has an end as well as a beginning.

Nicolas Walter

Death is natural. Without it there would be no life.

A little while and you will be nobody
nowhere, nor will anything which you
now see exist, nor any of those now alive.
Nature's law is that all things change
and turn, and pass away, so that in due
course, different things may be.

Marcus Aurelius

And when it comes, it will even be
welcomed by many as an end to pain . . .

> Why do I think of Death
> As a friend?
> It is because he is a scatterer,
> He scatters the human frame
> The nerviness and the great pain,
> Throws it on the fresh fresh air
> And now it is nowhere
> Only sweet Death does this,
> Sweet Death, Kind Death,
> Of all the gods you are the best.

Stevie Smith

Would our lives now really be any better if we believed in another life to come?

It is confusing to even try to imagine what life after life might possibly be.

If we were disembodied, what sense could we make of things like love, experiences, communication, achievements, or the warmth of the sun on our face? Many humanists, although they might prefer to live longer than in fact they will, would also draw attention to the tedium that we would experience if we were immortal.

It is the fact of death that brings structure to our lives. It frames our existence on this earth. Without death, but with the prospect of eternal life instead, what could motivate us to do anything, to care for others, to seek achievements – what would be the point?

Take the idea that life can only have a meaning if it never ends. It is certainly not the case that in general only endless activities can be meaningful. Indeed, usually the contrary is true: there being some end or completion is often required for an activity to have any meaning.

Julian Baggini

Is it so small a thing
To have enjoy'd the sun,
To have lived light in the spring,
To have loved, to have thought, to have done;
To have advanced true friends, and beat down
    baffling foes;

That we must feign a bliss
Of doubtful future date,
And while we dream on this
Lose all our present state,
And relegate to worlds yet distant our repose?

Matthew Arnold

Imagine you are listening to a favourite piece of music. You're enjoying it. Maybe you're humming or singing along, tapping your foot, perhaps dancing a little. Then, just when the track is about to end, it skips back to the beginning and starts again. That's alright a couple of times. If it's one of your favourites, you don't mind hearing it again.

But it happens again. Then again. In fact, it never stops, the track never changes, and you are listening to it again and again and again, constantly on a loop.

Or imagine you're eating your favourite food. Your favourite flavour and plenty of it. The anticipation and then that first mouthful – delicious! Then the second mouthful and the whole thing a real treat from start to finish. Only there is no finish.

The dish is always full and you're always eating.

On and on and on.

How long before your favourite song is meaningless to you? How long before your once favourite treat becomes tasteless to you, maybe even makes you sick to your stomach?

Or imagine you are reading a novel. The characters are engaging, their relationships twist and turn and are full of interest. You can't wait to see how they turn out in the end. But there is no end. The story just goes on and on. There is no resolution. It never ends.

Things need to end if they are to be enjoyable. Would you really want to live for ever?

Often what people really want is not to live for ever but to live for as long as possible, in the best possible health, with friends around them, and with meaning.

Luckily, we have the power to do something about that!

A humanist wants to live well and physical health is part of this

We are lucky to be living at a time when we understand health and our own bodies more than ever before in history.

We can't rewrite our DNA and any genetic risks of disease that we may have inherited. Nor can we control the role that chance plays in developing disease. But we can give ourselves the best possible chance of being healthy, through making lifestyle choices that will help our bodies.

Six well-evidenced tips to help you live longer and stay healthy!

1. Don't eat too much

2. Eat a balanced diet with plenty of fruit and vegetables

3. Keep an eye on your weight

4. Get some exercise every day

5. Get enough sleep

6. Don't smoke

However you feel about it, death is still a fact

We need to think about mortality – *really* think about it – acknowledge and accept it.

An acknowledgement that we only have one life, and that our lives are relatively short, can make many of humanity's differences and squabbles seem rather pointless.

It can be frightening to contemplate death – but it's a fact. Some people may find this a bit harsh, but reality is better faced than avoided.

Once we've accepted death, we can get on with living.

Perhaps the whole root of our trouble, the human trouble, is that we will sacrifice all the beauty of our lives, will imprison ourselves in totems, taboos, crosses, blood sacrifices, steeples, mosques, races, armies, flags, nations, in order to deny the fact of death, which is the only fact we have.

James Baldwin

I was not and was conceived.
I loved, and did a little work.
I am not, and grieve not.

W.K. Clifford

When I have fears, as Keats had fears,
Of the moment I'll cease to be,
I console myself with vanished years,
Remembered laughter, remembered tears,
And the peace of the changing sea.

Noel Coward

What we often think about when we think about death is not our own death but the death of those we love.

So this is not really about death. It is about loss, and indeed our sense of loss at such times can be overwhelming.

But the feeling of grief is the price of love.

Which would you rather have? Would you rather never have any love in your life – or would you rather love, even though this means you will inevitably experience loss and grief as a result?

When we lose someone we love, we know they have not 'gone to a better place'. They no longer exist in any physical sense.

And yet, for us left behind, the traces of their lives persist in myriad ways, from their descendants, to the deeds they have done, and in our memories of them. We can still speak with them in our own minds and – quite often – we know exactly how they would reply to us.

We carry their legacy forward in the human story – just as the people coming after us will do when we are gone.

To die completely, a person must not only forget but be forgotten, and he who is not forgotten is not dead.

Samuel Butler

It's uncomfortable to imagine the people we love so much as simply dead. But we can still take them on with us, with their genes and the lessons they taught us.

Ellie Harrison

Thomas Hardy was a Victorian novelist and is famous for books like *Tess of the D'Urbervilles* and *Jude the Obscure*. In the time when he lived, many people were rejecting the Christian worldview they had been raised with. He rejected it himself.

Instead of believing that human beings could live on in an afterlife, his work emphasised the connections that human generations have with each other.

> I am the family face;
> Flesh perishes, I live on,
> Projecting trait and trace
> Through time to times anon,
> And leaping from place to place
> Over oblivion.
>
> The years-heired feature that can
> In curve and voice and eye
> Despise the human span
> Of durance – that is I;
> The eternal thing in man,
> That heeds no call to die.

Thomas Hardy

Think about what you will leave behind when you are gone. What might others say you have contributed to their lives or to society?

Think about what others have left behind in you – the memories, the influence, the impact – that is how they live on.

Life is a relay race. Pass the baton on.

David Nobbs

Think of those you care about, imagine them mourning when you die, and ask yourself, how much sorrow you would wish them to bear. The answer would surely be: neither too much, nor for too long. You would wish them to come to terms with loss, and thereafter to remember the best of the past with joy, and you would wish them to continue life hopefully, which is the natural sentiment of the human condition.

If that is what we wish for those we will leave behind us when we die, then that is what we must believe would be desired by those who have already died. In that way we do justice to a conception of what their best and kindest wishes for us would be, and thereby, begin to restore the balance that is upset by this most poignant of life's sorrows.

A.C. Grayling

An individual human existence should be like a river – small at first, narrowly contained within its banks, and rushing passionately past boulders and over waterfalls. Gradually the river grows wider, the banks recede, the waters flow more quietly, and – in the end – without any visible break, they become merged in the sea, and painlessly lose their individual being. The man or woman who in old age, can see his or her life in this way, will not suffer from the fear of death, since the things they care for will continue.

Bertrand Russell

Now the land that I knew is a dream
And the line on the distance grows faint
So wide is my river
The horizon a sliver
The artist has run out of paint
Where the blue of the sea meets the sky
And the big yellow sun leads me home
I'm everywhere now
The way is a vow
To the wind of each breath by and by
The water sustains me without even trying
The water can't drown me, I'm done
With my dying

Johnny Flynn and Laura Marling

We are going to die, and that makes us the lucky ones.

Most people are never going to die because they are never going to be born.

The potential people who could have been here in my place but who will in fact never see the light of day outnumber the sand grains of Arabia.

Richard Dawkins

living well

There is no end to the adventures that
we can have if only we seek them with
our eyes open.

Jawaharlal Nehru

We only live once

This is not a drill. There is no second life to come.

Even the future in this one life is unpredictable and there are no guarantees about what will happen next.

So it makes sense to enjoy life now.

The meaning of life is to live it, as wholly as we can, as abundantly as we can, as bravely as we can, here and now, sharing the experience with others, caring for others as we care for ourselves, and accepting our responsibility for leaving the world better than we found it.

James Hemming

Loveliest of trees, the cherry now
Is hung with bloom along the bough,
And stands about the woodland ride
Wearing white for Eastertide
Now, of my threescore years and ten,
Twenty will not come again,
And take from seventy springs a score,
It only leaves me fifty more.
And since to look at things in bloom
Fifty springs are little room,
About the woodlands I will go
To see the cherry hung with snow.

A.E. Housman

For a humanist, there is no single meaning of life.

The universe has no ultimate direction or purpose.

Meaning is not something waiting out there to be discovered like a natural law or a distant star.

Meaning is something that *we* create.

We give meaning to our experience and we find fulfilment and happiness in what we do in our lives.

The purpose of life is to live it, to taste experience to the utmost, to reach out eagerly and without fear for newer and richer experience.

Eleanor Roosevelt

**Living well for a humanist is about seeking fulfil-
ment and helping others to do the same.**

This fulfilment comes from our connections. Our connections with fellow human beings – friends, family and others – and with the natural world.

It also comes from our pursuits, the exercise of our curiosity, our appreciation of beauty in all its forms, and our sense of wonder.

There are as many potential good and meaningful lives as there are people.

To love justice, to long for the right; to love mercy,
to pity the suffering, to assist the weak, to forget
wrongs and remember benefits; to love the truth, to
be sincere, to utter honest words; to love liberty, to
wage relentless war against slavery in all its forms;
to love wife or husband, and child, and friend, to
make a happy home; to love the beautiful in art,
in nature, to cultivate the mind; to be familiar with
the mighty thoughts that genius has expressed, the
noble deeds of all the world; to cultivate courage
and cheerfulness, to make others happy; to fill life
with the splendour of generous acts, the warmth of
loving words; to discard error, to destroy prejudice,
to receive new truths with gladness; to cultivate
hope, to see the calm beyond the storm, the dawn
beyond the night; to do the best that can be done
and then to be resigned . . .

Robert G. Ingersoll

Our relationships with others are a key ingredient of the good life.

We are warmed by the joys of love and family and friendship and close relationships. We gain comfort and security from the sense of being part of a wider community. Working with others to create a better world, we can find purpose in widening our interests beyond the limits of our own individual lives to improve the lives of others.

One's life has value so long as one attributes value to the life of others, by means of love, friendship, indignation, and compassion.

Simone de Beauvoir

I would like to live to the full, right now, and I hope that I live in such a way that the world is a little bit better after I leave it than it was when I arrived.

Philip Pullman

Virtue is attended by more peace of mind than vice, and meets with a more favourable reception from the world. I am sensible, that, according to the past experience of mankind, friendship is the chief joy of human life and moderation the only source of tranquillity and happiness.

David Hume

Epicurus lived just over 2,300 years ago in Athens, where he established a community known as his Garden. There, he and his friends – who extremely unusually for his time included women and slaves – lived as equals.

The teachings of Epicurus inspired many generations of people in ancient Europe for nearly a thousand years until they were mostly wiped out by Christians. Today, humanists find inspiration in his words, some surviving in their original form, with others quoted by later writers. Wonderfully, archaeologists have managed to recover some fragments of Epicurus' works – preserved in charred scrolls from Herculaneum. With the advent of advanced scientific imaging techniques, it may be possible to retrieve even more in the not-too-distant future.

Followers of Epicurus' example didn't believe that there were any gods that were interested in human affairs. They believed that human life had come about by natural processes, and that happiness should be the aim of life. Happiness, they believed, would come from calm moderation, behaving justly and from friendship.

Good advice from Epicurus

Nothing satisfies the person who is not satisfied
with a little. To want more and to be envious of
others means only competition and endless mental
distress, all to no purpose. But nature's wealth
is easy to get, and is enough for us to live a
complete and full life tranquilly.

Death is nothing to us. All pleasure and pain
consists in feeling, but death is the lack of feeling.

Of all the things which a wise person acquires
in pursuit of the happy and complete life, far the
greatest is friendship.

The arts in all their forms – paintings, music, novels and poems, films and plays – are essential to our lives.

They sharpen our awareness, enrich our understanding of the world and open our eyes to its beauty. They hold up a mirror to our own past and current experiences and open us up to new perspectives and different ways of being.

Have you ever been sad and felt like listening to a sad song? It is a profound moment to have what were your own private thoughts expressed in a beautiful way by someone else. Art and stories can show us things outside of our own experience, helping us to understand our own emotions better on reflection.

Art – any kind of art – can give us more clarity about our own thoughts and feelings, connect us with others, and teach us something about ourselves and them.

The poet Percy Shelley once said: 'Poets are the unacknowledged legislators of the world.' So much of our shared understanding of the world around us has been given shape and clarity by great thinkers and artists.

Literature is where I go to explore the highest and lowest places in human society and in the human spirit, where I hope to find not absolute truth but the truth of the tale, of the imagination of the heart.

Salman Rushdie

My horizon on humanity is enlarged by reading the writers of poems, seeing a painting, listening to some music, some opera, which has nothing at all to do with a volatile human condition or struggle or whatever. It enriches me as a human being.

Wole Soyinka

The best moments in reading are when you come across something – a thought, a feeling, a way of looking at things – which you had thought special and particular to you. Now here it is, set down by someone else, a person you have never met, someone even who is long dead. And it is as if a hand has come out and taken yours.

Alan Bennett

Take time just to be

In a moment, sit somewhere comfortable and close your eyes.

Try and sit like this for a few minutes.

Congratulations – you have just meditated. Meditation has been practised in religious and non-religious ways for thousands of years. You don't have to be a dedicated student of meditation to enjoy some of its benefits.

People tend to find they feel better and can think more clearly as a result of having these little moments of quiet.

If we spent half an hour every day in silent immobility, I am convinced that we should conduct all our affairs, personal, national, and international, far more sanely than we do at present.

Bertrand Russell

Connect with the natural world, its beauty, its diversity and its richness.

Keep close to Nature's heart . . . and break clear
away, once in a while, and climb a mountain
or spend a week in the woods. Wash your
spirit clean.

John Muir

Only by walking hand in hand with nature, only by
a reverent and loving study of the mysteries forever
around us, is it possible to disabuse the mind of the
narrow view, the contracted belief that time is now
and eternity tomorrow. Eternity is today.

The goldfinches and the tiny caterpillars, the
brilliant sun, if looked at lovingly and thoughtfully,
will lift the soul out of the smaller life of human
care that is of selfish aims, bounded by seventy
years, into the greater, the limitless life which has
been going on over universal space from endless
ages past, which is going on now, and which
will forever and forever, in one form, or another,
continue to proceed.

Richard Jefferies

Get moving!

Physical exercise is not only important for maintaining a generally healthy body – it is good for your mind as well. There's evidence that regular exercise can help both to prevent and relieve depression.

Physical activity has positive effects on emotion, sleep and appetite. It doesn't seem to matter too much what sort of physical activity you do – so find something you enjoy and indulge yourself. You'll be happier and healthier as a result.

Who is happy?

The one with a healthy body

and a ready mind.

Thales of Miletus

Give free rein to your curiosity

Curiosity is right at the heart of being human. Curiosity leads us to examine ourselves and wonder who we are and where we come from. Curiosity produces extraordinary journeys of creative discovery and great art. Curiosity leads us to ask questions which motivate scientific investigation.

Many religions contain warnings about curiosity: don't ask too many questions; don't ask for evidence; don't allow yourself to doubt.

But for humanists, curiosity is a virtue.

I think, at a child's birth, if a mother could ask a fairy godmother to endow it with the most useful gift, that gift would be curiosity.

Eleanor Roosevelt

Curiosity begets love. It weds us to the world. It's part of our perverse, madcap love for this impossible planet we inhabit. People die when curiosity goes. People have to find out, people have to know.

Graham Swift

Give free rein to your creativity

Creativity is another human aptitude that can make us feel fulfilled and help us to connect with other people. Wherever your creativity lies – in drawing, painting, music, writing, conversing, gardening or anything else – enjoy this wonderful part of being human.

Albert Einstein said, 'Imagination is more important than knowledge. Knowledge is limited. Imagination encircles the world.'

Creativity is a hugely important part of my life and it's important for my mental health. It's important for my understanding of the world and the things that happen, and things that happen to me, and the decisions I'm making, and everything else, I can't really overstate that.

There are times when it's immensely frustrating because you know there's a moment when the song doesn't exist and then you get this feeling of what the finished song will feel like and sound like and getting from that moment to the actual finished thing, it can be a short and breezy and wonderful journey, and it can be an absolute nightmare that takes years. But that kind of frustration is also the most exciting part as well.

There are moments when it's like when you're cutting wrapping paper and the scissors start to glide. There are moments when the songwriting starts to glide and that's the best feeling in the world.

Frank Turner

Give free rein to love

We can love not just those around us, not just friends and family, or even the strangers we might meet, but extend our love to the whole of humanity.

We can embrace kindness and compassion, fairness and justice, honesty and integrity, not as imposed obligations to which we must conform, but as qualities which enrich our lives and our relationships with others.

One person alone is not a full person: we exist in relation to others.

Margaret Atwood

Happiness is the only good, the time to be happy is now, and the way to be happy is to make others so.

Robert G. Ingersoll

We can't just sit around waiting for things to happen to us. If we want happiness in our lives, we must get up and go for it.

That isn't to say our fate is entirely in our own hands – it isn't. But we certainly won't get anywhere if we don't try.

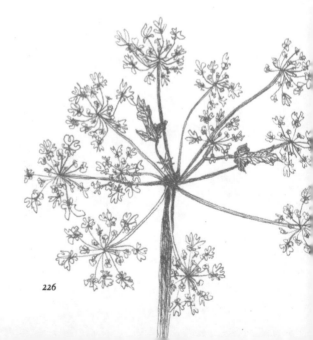

It will never rain roses: when we want
to have more roses, we must plant
more trees.

George Eliot

Our lives are less than a thousand months
long and to make the best of it we need
to have fun, form strong friendships and
make the best of the gifts we have.

A.C. Grayling

The word 'spiritual' is a difficult one for many people because it has so many different uses today. But if it refers to the inner life which enriches our existence, then those who do not believe in the supernatural have it as much as anyone else.

Many humanists recognise it as one of the greatest capacities of the human mind.

There are objects and occasions which invoke in me a profound sense of the sacred, and I can cite other humanist scientists of whom this is also true . . . Why, when you go to the Grand Canyon and you see the strata of geological time laid out before you, is there a feeling that brings you close to tears? Or looking at images from the Hubble telescope. I think it's no different from the feeling of being moved to tears by music, by a Schubert quartet, say, or by poetry. The human mind is big enough, and imaginative enough, to be poetically moved by the whole sweep of geological ages represented by the rocks that you are standing among. That's why you feel in awe.

Richard Dawkins

You are what you make of yourselves. Aim high, aim for the stars, and you may yet clear the rooftops. You will need courage, tenacity, motivation and a good sense of humour on the route. Quality of character, happiness, fulfilment of potential and of human needs can be improved through changed values, through redirection of individual life, by a process of personal change, and personal evolution.

Jeaneane Fowler

Should we choose 'freedom from' or 'freedom to'? The safe cage or the dangerous wild? Comfort, inertia, and boredom, or activity, risk, and peril? Being human and therefore of mixed motives, we want both; though, as a rule, alternately.

Margaret Atwood

Choose your own adventure

If you were reading the book of your life, what would you want to happen next?

Are there things you wish you could do, things you would like to say, places you wish you could go?

Do those things, say those things, go to those places! You are not reading your story, you're writing it. You're writing it even this minute.

Of course, you can't control every twist of the plot. And there will be sad and painful moments along the way – they're part of every story.

But you know where you've come from. You know where you're going to. There will be love and laughter and joy whatever else there will be.

Put down this book and step back into your own. The choices there are yours to make, they're waiting for you, and you have all you need to make them.

Humanist ceremonies
– marking life's events

When it comes to marking important events in our lives, more and more people are turning away from tired and outdated religious ceremonies, which don't capture their beliefs or values, and choosing humanist ceremonies instead.

Humanist ceremonies are carried out all around the world. Most are naming ceremonies, weddings and funerals. The charity, Humanists UK, has been helping people to create and carry out non-religious ceremonies since 1896, and today, humanist ceremonies are available in many countries, including Canada, the US, Australia, New Zealand, Norway and Iceland. Since the beginning of the twenty-first century, the demand for humanist ceremonies has grown enormously, with increasing awareness of this option and as non-religious people feel emboldened to make a choice that genuinely reflects their own beliefs and values.

In contrast with religious ceremonies, the central difference in a humanist ceremony is the absence of any reference to a deity. This creates a profoundly significant shift of focus and of purpose – in each case, it is the person who has died, the couple getting married or the baby who has been born that is put at the centre of the ritual. At the same time, the whole community of family and friends is invested with the responsibility of 'bearing witness' – *humanising*, instead of, as was previously the case, sanctifying the experience.

Humanist celebrants have described their work as 'an intimate, challenging and profoundly reward-ing act of creation'. Each ceremony is tailored to be personal and meaningful to the people involved and provides an opportunity to express the con-nections that are important to us in our lives. Humanists see relationships with other people as central to our human experience – and it is these relationships that are often at the heart of a humanist ceremony.

A humanist celebrant is someone who works closely with the people at the centre of a ceremony to help create an event that is unique, specific and meaningful to the people involved. This involves spending time with, and learning about, the people at the heart of the ceremony in order to help tell their story – or, at a naming ceremony, to celebrate the beginning of that story. Rather than follow-ing a set script, each script will be unique to that particular ceremony.

humanistceremonies.org.uk

The authors will be donating their profits from the sale of the book to Humanists UK, who support the training of more humanist celebrants and pastoral carers in hospitals and prisons in the UK.

About the humanists quoted

Douglas Adams (1952–2001) was an author, dramatist and satirist

Jim Al-Khalili (b.1962) is a scientist, writer, and a vice president and former president of Humanists UK

Kwame Anthony Appiah (b.1954) is a philosopher and novelist

Matthew Arnold (1822–1888) was a poet, critic and school inspector

Isaac Asimov (1920–1992) was a biochemist and author

David Attenborough (b.1926) is a naturalist, broadcaster and environmental activist

Margaret Atwood (b.1939) is a poet, author, environmental activist and was named American Humanist of the Year in 1987

A.J. Ayer (1910–1989) was a philosopher and president of Humanists UK

Julian Baggini (b.1968) is a philosopher, writer and patron of Humanists UK

James Baldwin (1924–1987) was a novelist, essayist and activist for justice

Kristen Bell (b.1980) is an actor, most famous for *The Good Place*

Alan Bennett (b.1934) is a playwright and author

Jeremy Bentham (1748–1832) was a philosopher and social reformer

Aneurin Bevan (1897–1960) was a politician who created the UK's National Health Service

William Beveridge (1879–1963) was an economist, politician and social reformist

Simon Blackburn (b.1944) is a philosopher, writer and patron of Humanists UK

Harold Blackham (1903–2009) was a writer, philosopher, educationalist and a chief executive of Humanists UK

Fenner Brockway (1888–1988) was a politician, an activist for racial equality and peace, and patron of Humanists UK

Jacob Bronowski (1908–1974) was a scientist, writer, broadcaster and patron of Humanists UK

John Bagnell Bury (1861–1927) was a classical scholar and historian

Samuel Butler (1835–1902) was a novelist and philosopher

Brock Chisholm (1898–1967) was the first director-general of the World Health Organization

W.K. Clifford (1845–1879) was a mathematician and philosopher

Alexander Comfort (1920–2000) was a physician and author

Confucius (551–479 BCE) is the Latinised name of Kong Fuzi, who was a philosopher and social leader

Noel Coward (1899–1973) was a composer, playwright, actor, director and singer

Jo Cox (1974–2016) was a politician, internationalist and member of the UK Parliament's humanist group

Marie Curie (1867–1934) was a physicist and chemist and the first female Nobel laureate

Charles Darwin (1809–1882) was a naturalist best known for developing the theory of evolution by natural selection

Richard Dawkins (b.1941) is a scientist, writer and patron of Humanists UK

Simone de Beauvoir (1908–1986) was a philosopher, activist, author and feminist

Albert Einstein (1879–1959) was a physicist, activist for peace and internationalism, and member of a number of humanist societies

George Eliot (1819–1880) was the pen name of Mary Ann Evans, a novelist, journalist and essayist

Epicurus (341–270 BCE) was a philosopher and founder of a commune

E.M. Forster (1879–1970) was a novelist, broadcaster, liberal activist and patron of Humanists UK

Jeaneane Fowler is a sociologist and scholar of
humanism

Rosalind Franklin (1920–1958) was a chemist whose
work led to the understanding of DNA

Stephen Fry (b.1957) is an actor, writer and patron of
Humanists UK

Ricky Gervais (b.1961) is an actor, writer and patron
of Humanists UK

Stephen Jay Gould (1941–2002) was a biologist and
writer

A.C. Grayling (b.1949) is a philosopher, writer,
teacher and vice president of Humanists UK

J.B.S. Haldane (1892–1964) was a scientist and
mathematician

Lorraine Hansberry (1930–1965) was a playwright
and essayist

Thomas Hardy (1840–1928) was a novelist and poet

Ellie Harrison (b.1977) is a naturalist, television
presenter and activist for wildlife conservation

Eustace Haydon (1880–1975) was a historian and
humanist leader

James Hemming (1909–2007) was a psychologist,
education campaigner and president of
Humanists UK

A.E. Housman (1859–1936) was a classical scholar
and poet

Humanists International (founded 1952) is the global umbrella body bringing together national humanist organisations

David Hume (1711–1776) was a philosopher, historian, essayist and economist

Zora Neale Hurston (1891–1960) was a writer and an important figure in the Harlem Renaissance

Aldous Huxley (1894–1963) was a writer and philosopher

Julian Huxley (1887–1975) was an evolutionary biologist who co-founded Humanists International, and served as the first president of Humanists UK and first director-general of UNESCO

Robert G. Ingersoll (1833–1899) was a humanist activist and lawyer

Richard Jefferies (1848–1887) was an author

John Maynard Keynes (1883–1946) was an economist

Margaret Knight (1903–1983) was a psychologist, writer and patron of Humanists UK

Jennie Lee (1904–1988) was a politician and founder of the Open University

Lucretius (c.94–55 BCE) was a philosopher and poet

Marcus Aurelius (121–180 CE) was emperor of Rome and a philosopher

Peter Mayer is a singer and songwriter

Margaret Mead (1901–1978) was a cultural anthropologist and author

Peter Medawar (1915–1987) was a biologist, immunologist and author

Mencius (372–289 BCE) is the Latinised name of Mengzhi, who was a philosopher and political adviser

John Stuart Mill (1806–1873) was a philosopher and politician

John Muir (1838–1914) was a naturalist, author, philosopher and early advocate for the preservation of wilderness in the US

Jawaharlal Nehru (1889–1964) was an activist for an independent India and its first prime minister

David Nobbs (1935–2015) was a comic writer best known as the creator of Reginald Perrin and a patron of Humanists UK

Richard Norman (b.1943) is a moral philosopher and patron of Humanists UK

Diana Nyad (b.1949) is a record-breaking marathon swimmer

John Boyd Orr (1880–1971) was a teacher, scientist, politician and winner of the Nobel Peace Prize

George Orwell (1903–1950) was a journalist, novelist, essayist and broadcaster

Steven Pinker (b.1954) is a cognitive psychologist, linguist and author

Karl Popper (1902–1994) was a philosopher and patron of Humanists UK

Jaap van Praag (1911–1981) was a counsellor and founder of the Dutch Humanist League

Terry Pratchett (1948–2015) was an author, satirist and patron of Humanists UK

Protagoras (490–420 BCE) was a philosopher

Publius Papinius Statius (c.45–96 CE) was a poet

Philip Pullman (b.1946) is a novelist, essayist and patron of Humanists UK

Carl Rogers (1902–1987) was a psychologist and a founder of the humanistic approach to counselling

Eleanor Roosevelt (1884–1962) was a diplomat and human rights activist

Manabendra Nath ('M.N.') Roy (1887–1954) was a revolutionary activist, political theorist and philosopher

Salman Rushdie (b.1947) is a novelist, essayist and patron of Humanists UK

Bertrand Russell (1872–1970) was a philosopher, writer, activist for peace, patron of Humanists UK and winner of the Nobel Literature Prize

Adam Rutherford (b.1975) is a geneticist, author, broadcaster and patron of Humanists UK

Carl Sagan (1934–1996) was a cosmologist and populariser of science

Jean-Paul Sartre (1905–1980) was a philosopher, playwright, author and activist

Amartya Sen (b.1933) is a philosopher, economist and a former patron of Humanists UK

William Shakespeare (1564–1616) was an actor, playwright and poet

George Bernard Shaw (1856–1950) was a playwright and activist

Mary Shelley (1797–1851) was a writer and editor

Peter Singer (b.1946) is a philosopher, one of the intellectual founders of the modern animal rights movement and was Australian Humanist of the Year in 2004

Stevie Smith (1902–1971) was a poet and novelist

Zadie Smith (b.1975) is a novelist and essayist

Wole Soyinka (b.1934) is a playwright, poet and essayist. He was the first African to win the Nobel Prize for Literature and was named International Humanist of the Year in 2014

Gloria Steinem (b.1935) is a journalist and activist who led the way in advocating equal rights for women in the US

Leslie Stephen (1832–1904) was an author, historian and mountaineer

Graham Swift (b.1949) is a novelist

Thales of Miletus (c.623–c.545 BCE) was a philosopher

Emma Thompson (b.1959) is an actor, writer and human rights activist

Lionel Trilling (1905–1975) was a literary critic and author

Frank Turner (b.1981) is a musician and patron of Humanists UK

The United Nations (founded 1945) is an intergovernmental organisation founded to promote peace and security

Kurt Vonnegut (1922–2007) was a novelist and president of the American Humanist Association

Nicolas Walter (1934–2000) was a journalist, activist for peace and patron of Humanists UK

Janet Whitaker (b.1936) is a politician and patron of Humanists UK

Mary Wollstonecraft (1759–1797) was a philosopher, writer and activist for women's rights

Xenophanes (c.570–c.475 BCE) was a philosopher and poet

About the illustrators and photographers

Anna Cooley worked in natural history TV programming in London before starting a family in the late 1990s. In 2003 she and her husband, the sculptor Simon Cooley, moved to rural Wales and set up a sculpture workshop business which they still run from their home each summer. Anna has been drawing every day since an accident forced temporary immobility in 2018. She now splits her time between running the business and hospitality side of their summer workshops and pursuing her career in art and illustration. She finds joy and inspiration in her surroundings: walking in the hills with her dog Mr Pepys, cooking, and spending time with family and friends. She is greatly amused by her feathered friends – guinea fowl, Runner ducks and Pekin bantams – which are the subject of many of her drawings.

Anna's illustrations are featured on pp. 23, 49, 70, 83, 85, 93, 105, 111, 119, 125, 130, 136, 147, 149, 171, 191, 207, 222, 226.

Wendy Slade grew up in a family that nurtured a curiosity of the world in which we live. It was common practice for her own and previous generations to carry a sketchbook and record their love of nature and fascination with urban or natural environments and their inhabitants through illustrations and paintings. This is something Wendy now fosters in her own family and believes encourages respect and understanding of our shared world. Wendy went to art college, but subsequently pursued studies in linguistics then information management. These days she ensures that her career as an academic development manager in higher education is balanced with a good dose of art, live music, walks and cake with family and friends.

Wendy's illustrations are featured on pp. 15, 18, 45, 66, 69, 110, 141, 193, 201, 216, 219, 232.

Natasha Vdovkina is a Bristol-based therapist and photographer. Her love of photography started in early childhood. Born in Russia, she remembers fondly developing films at home with her father during cold, dark winter months. Looking through old photographs is still her favourite pastime. Natasha is drawn to colour, low light, connection between people and emotion. She enjoys portraiture, landscape and lifestyle photography. Her inspiration comes from travelling, studying art and life stories she gets to hear in her counselling practice.

About the authors

Andrew Copson has been chief executive of Humanists UK since 2009 and president of Humanists International since 2015. He has provided a humanist voice on many television and radio programmes, and written on humanism in many outlets in print and online. He finds joy and meaning in promoting humanism, spending time with his family and cavapoo, gardening, reading novels, ancient history and walking in the woods.

Alice Roberts is a biological anthropologist. She's written many books and has fronted many television series – about science, anthropology and archaeology – on the BBC and Channel 4. She has been Professor of Public Engagement in Science at the University of Birmingham since 2012. Alice was awarded Humanist of the Year in 2015 for her efforts to promote the teaching of evolution – and resisting biblical creationism – in schools. In 2019, she became president of Humanists UK, and she promotes humanism as a positive, non-religious philosophy in her 'humanist mini-sermons' on Twitter. She finds joy and meaning in sharing ideas, spending time with family and friends, making art, and connecting with nature – walking, cycling and kayaking. Some of her illustrations and photographs also appear among these pages: pp. 21, 25, 29, 38, 41, 43, 51, 55, 59, 65, 78, 81, 86, 94, 98, 107, 109, 124, 133, 144, 151, 153, 158, 163, 168, 172, 175, 177, 183, 185, 189, 195, 203, 215, 221, 225, 227, 229.

Acknowledgements

Thank you to the staff and volunteers of Humanists UK and the humanists of Twitter for their help and support in finding so many great humanist quotes. Keep them coming!

Copyright and references

pp.11 Kurt Vonnegut, *God Bless You, Mr Rosewater*, Vintage 1992; 13 *Life* magazine, 1988; 15 'Blue Boat Home' lyrics written by Peter Mayer, copyright 2002. www.petermayer.net; 17 Jeaneanne Fowler, *Humanism*, Sussex Academic Press 1999; 26 Zora Neale Hurston, *Dust Tracks on a Road*, Harper Perennial Modern Classics 2006; 29 *Think RE: Pupil Book 3*, Pearson 2005; 30 Peter Singer, *The Expanding Circle*, Princeton 2011; 39 *The Wiley Blackwell Handbook of Humanism*, Wiley-Blackwell 2015; 47 Carl Rogers, *On Becoming A Person*, Constable 2004; 49 Jeaneanne Fowler, *Humanism*; 50 Adam Rutherford, *The Book of Humans*, W&N 2018; 57 Kwame Anthony Appiah, 'There is no such thing as western civilisation', *Guardian* 9 Nov 2016; 61 Gloria Steinem, Address to the Women of America at the founding of the National Women's Political Caucus, 1971; 67 The Bertrand Russell Peace Foundation Ltd; 70 Steven Pinker, *The Better Angels of Our Nature*, Penguin 2012; 71 Amartya Sen, *The Idea of Justice*, Penguin 2010; 83 World Humanist Day tweet, 2018 https://twitter.com/rickygervais/status/1009879236662972418;

95 'Hot Ones' YouTube interview, Aug 2018; 99 The Bertrand Russell Peace Foundation Ltd; 101 *What is Humanism?*, Wayland 2018; 116–7 The Bertrand Russell Peace Foundation Ltd; 121 Jeaneanne Fowler, *Humanism*; 125 Stevie Smith, 'The Past', *Selected Poems*, Penguin Modern Classics 2002; 136, Zadie Smith, *White Teeth*, Penguin 2001; 142–3 Carl Sagan, *The Demon-Haunted World*, Ballantine Books 1995; 151 © Lorraine Hansberry, 2001, *A Raisin in the Sun*, Methuen Drama, an imprint of Bloomsbury Publishing Plc.; 153 Carl Sagan, *The Demon-Haunted World*; 154 Graham Swift, *Waterland*, Scribner 2019; 157 'Wild, wild life', *Sydney Morning Herald*, 24 Mar 2003; 159 George Orwell, 'Lear, Tolstoy and the Fool', *Inside the Whale and Other Essays*, Penguin 2001; 160 Zora Neale Hurston, *Dust Tracks on a Road*; 168 The Bertrand Russell Peace Foundation Ltd; 171 Letter to the *Guardian*, 16 Sep 1993; 173 Stevie Smith, 'When One', *Selected Poems*, Penguin Modern Classics 2002; 175 Julian Baggini, *Atheism: A Very Short Introduction*, OUP 2003; 183 'Letter from a Region of My Mind', *The New Yorker* 17 Nov 1962; 184 © Noel Coward, 2007, *Noel Coward Collected Verse* (New Edition), Methuen Drama, an imprint of Bloomsbury Publishing Plc.; 190 'The Last Word on Sorrow', *Guardian*, 16 Oct 1999; 192 The Bertrand Russell Peace Foundation Ltd; 193 'The Water', Johnny Flynn feat. Laura Marling, Transgressive Records 2010; 205 The Bertrand Russell Peace Foundation Ltd; 213 Alan Bennett, *The History Boys*, Faber 2004; 215 The Bertrand Russell Peace Foundation Ltd; 221 Graham Swift, *Waterland*; 229 'Is nothing sacred?', speech at the 2001 Humanist Philoso-phers' conference; 230–1 Jeaneanne Fowler, *Humanism*; 232 Margaret Atwood, *Freedom*, Vintage 2018

Humanists UK

At Humanists UK, we want a tolerant world where rational thinking and kindness prevail. We work to support lasting change for a better society, championing ideas for the one life we have, drawing on contemporary humanist thought and the worldwide humanist tradition.

Our work helps people to be happier and more fulfilled, and by bringing non-religious people together we help them develop their own views and an understanding of the world around them.

We're committed to putting humanism into practice. Through our ceremonies, pastoral support, education services, and campaigning work, we advance free thinking and freedom of choice so everyone can live in a fair and equal society.

Since 1896, we've always been a growing movement at the forefront of social change. If you want to support us in our work, please do join or donate. We are dependent on charitable giving to continue our work.

Find out more at our website, at <u>humanists.uk.</u>

Humanists UK, 39 Moreland Street, London EC1V 8BB. Registered charity in England and Wales no. 285987 and company limited by guarantee no. 228781.